Facing Trials:
Thoughts For Meditation

Cheryl Zelenka

Copyright © 2013 Cheryl Zelenka.

All rights reserved. No part of this book may be used or reproduced by any means, graphic, electronic, or mechanical, including photocopying, recording, taping or by any information storage retrieval system without the written permission of the publisher except in the case of brief quotations embodied in critical articles and reviews.

Author Credits:
1) Christain Focus Magazine (04/2013)
http://www.christianfocusmag.com/subscribe-christian-focus
2) FaithWriters A Devotional "He Knows My Frame" (3-20-13)
http://www.faithwriters.com/member-profile.php?id=61840
3) Faithful Bloggers: http://faithful

WestBow Press books may be ordered through booksellers or by contacting:

WestBow Press
A Division of Thomas Nelson
1663 Liberty Drive
Bloomington, IN 47403
www.westbowpress.com
1-(866) 928-1240

Because of the dynamic nature of the Internet, any web addresses or links contained in this book may have changed since publication and may no longer be valid. The views expressed in this work are solely those of the author and do not necessarily reflect the views of the publisher, and the publisher hereby disclaims any responsibility for them.

Any people depicted in stock imagery provided by Thinkstock are models, and such images are being used for illustrative purposes only.

Certain stock imagery © Thinkstock.

ISBN: 978-1-4908-0740-9 (sc)
ISBN: 978-1-4908-0742-3 (hc)
ISBN: 978-1-4908-0741-6 (e)

Library of Congress Control Number: 2013916203

Printed in the United States of America.

WestBow Press rev. date: 9/10/2013

Table of Contents

Special Thanks xi
Foreword xiii

Chapter 1: Facing Trials 1
    Roll Over when Life Knocks You Down 2
    He Will Restore All the Years the Locusts
    Have Devoured 5
Chapter 2: Broken 7
    Broken Seed 8
    Broken, Then Reassembled 11
Chapter 3: Prayer 14
    Open the Eyes of My Heart, Lord 15
    Are Delays Denials from God? 18
Chapter 4: Obedience 21
    Our Obedience = Godly Results 22
    Obedience Leads to a Future Hope 25
Chapter 5: Obstacles 28
    About That Elephant in the Living Room 29
    Obstacles Can Change Our Heart 32
Chapter 6: Love 35
    Who Are the Unlovable? 36
    God Is a Gentleman 39
Chapter 7: Sin and Forgiveness 42
    The Potter and His Clay 43
    Nobody Is Beyond Forgiveness 46

Chapter 8: Transformation and Refining 49
    God Does Not Compare the Flowers in
    His Garden..50
    Pearls and Diamonds 53
Chapter 9: Endurance and Perseverance 55
    Don't Give Up! 56
    It Takes Endurance to Scale a Mountain of God 59
Chapter 10: Spiritual Path
    and Spiritual Journey 62
    Life in a Fog..63
    Looking Back Old Chapters vs. New Chapters......66
Chapter 11: Fear 69
    Fear Cripples and Trips Up the Believer..................70
    Fear Is a Prison 73
Chapter 12: Faith 76
    Shipwrecked and Broken, But Safe..............................77
    Keep Your Eyes on Jesus 80
Chapter 13: Free Will and God's Will? 83
    God's Will and His Willingness 84
    Stumbles, Skinned Knees, and Open Arms............87
Chapter 14: Healing 90
    "I'm Cracked, Lord, and I Need Healing!"............91
    God Will Heal Your Broken Pieces 94
Chapter 15: God's Plan and Purpose 97
    The Unique Ways and Thoughts of God..................98
    Don't Light the Fire When God Has the
    Matches!..100
Chapter 16: Control 103
    Who Is Leading the Procession?..................................104
    Don't Run Ahead of God..106
Chapter 17: Worry and Anxiety 108
    That Nasty Villain Named Worry 109

	The Anxiety of Mary	112
Chapter 18:	Hope	116
	There Is Always Hope	117
	Hope Will Move You Forward	120
Chapter 19:	Wisdom	123
	A Wise Person Knows When to Speak	124
	How to Obtain Wisdom	127
Chapter 20:	Walking with the Spirit of God	130
	Spiritual Maturity	131
	Confusion Is *Not* of the Lord	134
About the Author		137
Notes		139

Dedication

This book is dedicated to Barbara Ann Zelenka, my biggest fan, my darling mother, and a treasured blessing. Thank you for your constant, unconditional love and support.

Special Thanks

This book would not have been possible without the help, encouragement, wisdom, and support of Phil Fischer, Greg Holt, and Tina Carson. I wish to offer a special thanks to my second cousin Nancy Studebaker for her help in revising and editing this book. Paths cross for a reason.

Thanks to the following for permission to use graphics:

Michael Waters, for the cartoon: mike@joyfulcartoons.com
Sherly Electra from A God's Child: http://hearjesuschrist.blogspot.in/
Butch and Julie Rhodenizer, Wholly His, Inc., https://www.facebook.com/WhollyHis
Becky Capps from Trust Him Always: http://fb.com/TrustHimAlways

The following artists from All-Free Download & Pixabay:
Hans Braxmeier, James DeMers, Bart Glompie, G.Hodan, Petr Kratochvil,
Vera Kratochvil, Saulhm, and Ulrich Welzel,

Foreword

As a writer of encouraging words and articles that highlight the wisdom of God's Word, I appreciate finding other authors of like mind.

Several months ago as I was searching through the Christian blogs, I happened upon *Weeping into Dancing.* This was my introduction to Cheryl, the author of this wonderful book. Her devotionals blessed me!

Right away, I knew I had to invite her to be an author on my Christian blog; sure enough, I was rewarded with a *yes!*

It doesn't matter who we are, where we live, or what stage of life we are in—*we all face trials!* As human beings, we are always seeking *that one thing, that one person, that one moment,* hoping that once we find it, it will make our lives bearable, or even good again. Sadly, we often forget that we already possess that *one thing,* that "gotta have it" item. Only it is not a *thing.* And it is surely no item.

There is a hole in me, and there is one in you. Do you see it right there? This hole is meant to be filled by God. And this is where Cheryl shines.

Cheryl can take each place in our life and shine some light into it. Have you experienced depression or loss? Do you feel like the unlovable black sheep? Is fear a constant companion of yours? Maybe you are trying to get "right" with God again, or you simply need some encouragement.

Whatever your needs are, this book is the perfect companion to assist you in finding your way through the valley. Cheryl is uniquely qualified to encourage you and cheer you on as you walk with the Lord through it all.

And, if you are one who is blessed with few trials, this book will help you keep it that way! With Cheryl's down-to-earth insights wrapped up in real life instances, this book is easy to read and contains many great Scripture references.

I am also a writer. And I write not only to teach, but also to encourage people. So, when Cheryl asked me to write this foreword, I wasn't just honored, I thought it was a great idea! Everything Cheryl conveys in all of her writings has blessed me and countless others.

I pray that you will be blessed, comforted, and encouraged as you peruse Cheryl's insights and absorb the living Word of God in her new book, *Facing Trials: Thoughts for Meditation*.

—Greg Holt
Christian blogger and editor, *Vine of Life News*
(http://vineoflife.net/)
Marshfield, Wisconsin
May 2013

CHAPTER 1

FACING TRIALS

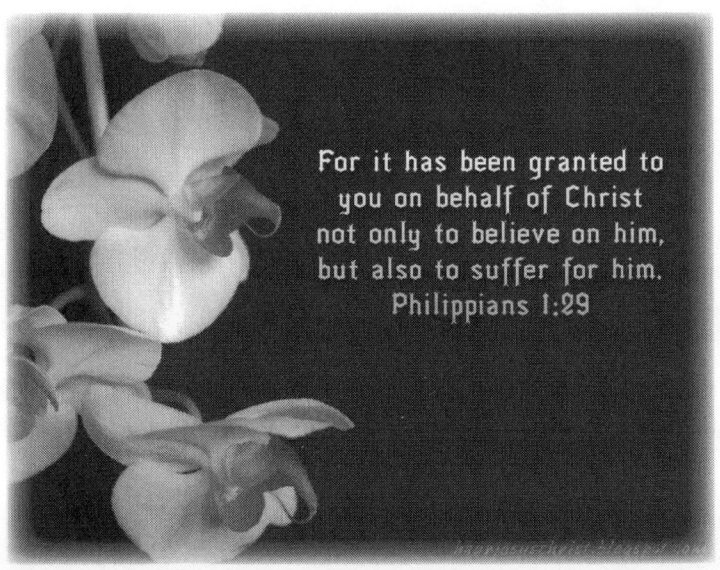

By Hear Jesus Christ

Roll Over when Life Knocks You Down

> Through affliction, He teaches us precious lessons that otherwise we would never learn. By affliction, He shows us our emptiness and weakness, draws us to the throne of grace, purifies our affections, weans us from the world and makes us long for heaven.[1]—J.C. Ryle

> Dear friends, do not be surprised at the fiery ordeal that has come on you to test you, as though something strange were happening to you. (1 Peter 4:12 NIV)

When difficult times knock you down, roll over and look up at the stars. It's okay if you don't have the strength to stand up right away. Facing unexpected trials can knock over even the most mature Christians. Reasons for a fall will differ from believer to believer. However, I do guarantee that Satan knows the vulnerable spots in every believer's armor and will not hesitate to aim fiery darts in his or her direction.

Trials are a part of life, and affliction usually accompanies them. Nobody can escape this. Joy and love, sorrow and hardships—these are what face us as we journey to our forever home after we die. We should try to accept that trials are part of our journeys in life and attempt to build up our spiritual muscles. We can do this by reading the Word of God.

In the first chapter of James, we are told to count trials as pure joy. How is this possible, and why is it a joyful thing to face difficulties? It is because the testing of your faith produces perseverance. When perseverance has finished its work, you will be mature in your faith, lacking nothing.

If you find yourself facedown in a puddle of mud and tears, you could drown! Roll over and gaze up at the heavens. Meditate on the constellations and imagine the one who designed it all. He is powerful. Better yet, He is powerful *and* loving. His compassions are new every morning. Tomorrow will be a fresh start. Romans 8:28 states, "And we know that in all things God works for the good of those who love Him, who have been called according to His purpose." Faith requires that you accept the truth of this Scripture, even though you may not see the good in your circumstances right now. God has a plan for your life, and He has allowed or sent your difficulty for a good reason.

Oswald Chambers wrote, "Hardships often prepare ordinary people for an extraordinary destiny."[2] Corrie ten Boom spent the first fifty years of her life learning lessons of love and forgiveness so that she could teach the world how to be more like Christ. God sent hardships her way and permitted trials in her life that transformed her character and refined her spirit.

Endurance and perseverance belong to the same family. They are cousins and true allies. Throughout your trial, you must hold on to the biblical fact that God will never leave you or forsake you. Your desert journey, or the hurricane you are experiencing, is only for a season. You will not live a life of sorrows. Your weeping will eventually turn into dancing. A joyful song will once again rise issue from your lips.

God loves to whisper words of hope and encouragement into the heart of a suffering and weary child. He walks with you through every one of your struggles.

So, while on your back, you will see the beauty of the night. Not all darkness is ugly and fearsome. Behold the lights God has provided in the darkest of times. A zillion pinpoints provide us with not only illumination, but also with the ability to navigate. It is true that in stormy weather it is harder to find your way, but storms do not last forever. If you are feeling lost, rest and wait for the weather to clear. Eventually, you will be able to navigate and continue on your journey. God will help you get back on your feet, but you have to will yourself to live and roll over.

Meditate on the three Bible verses below:

"When I consider Your heavens, the work of Your fingers, the moon and the stars, which You have set in place, what is mankind that You are mindful of them, human beings that You care for them? You have made them a little lower than the angels and crowned them with glory and honor" (Psalm 8:3-5 NIV).

"And God said, 'Let there be lights in the vault of the sky to separate the day from the night, and let them serve as signs to mark sacred times, and days and years, and let them be lights in the vault of the sky to give light on the earth.' And it was so" (Genesis 1:14-15 NIV).

"O Lord, by these things men live, and in all these is the life of my spirit. O restore me to health and make me live" (Isaiah 38:16 ESV)!

He Will Restore All the Years the Locusts Have Devoured

> I will repay you for the years the locusts have eaten—the great locust and the young locust, the other locusts and the locust swarm. (Joel 2:25 NIV)

Do you feel like you are stuck in a turbulent dust storm with no promise of fair weather in the near future? Is everything covered in dust and your vision greatly impaired? Has worry attempted to set her traps at night by throwing hopelessness into your dreams? Does she whisper into your ear, saying, "You have spent too much time wandering around lost in the dust and will never be able to finish your assigned work from God"?

What lies the Devil will invent to discourage and dissuade the children of God! You need to be grounded enough in your walk to recognize the nasty whisperings of the Enemy. To find your way out of the dust storm, you must get your eyes back on Jesus and off of your troubling circumstances.

God allows storms to strengthen your resolve so that you hold an ever-deepening conviction to move onward, toward Calvary. He knows how long you will struggle to weather your personal storm. He promises in Joel 2:25 to *restore* the years that the locusts have eaten. This means that while you are in a trial, the opportunities you miss out on or lose will be restored in His time. This is a promise.

You must first find your way out of the trial you are experiencing by learning the lessons God would have you understand. Be at peace in knowing that the world that has seemingly slipped past you is held in God's hands. Every minute of time you think has been lost is really *not* lost. God holds the stopwatch and is aware of your time line. He created it and has numbered your days.

Don't be afraid to venture down a path that seemingly eats up your time, fearful that you will never accomplish the goal set before you. God's purposes will always stand. He is faithful to complete the work that He has begun in you!

Finally, don't worry about the locusts. What you have lost is of little worth. Focus on laying up treasure in heaven. Recall the book of Job and remember that in the end of the story, God restores Job's wealth and increases all that he lost.

The Lord is not ignorant of your struggle. He has a reason for it, including a lesson for you to learn. He is all about equipping His children. You will be back on track soon and will be all the wiser, thanks to the dust storm God prepared for you to endure.

Below are three Bible passages for you to meditate on:

"When He had said this, Jesus called in a loud voice, 'Lazarus, come out!' The dead man came out, his hands and feet wrapped with strips of linen, and a cloth around his face. Jesus said to them, 'Take off the grave clothes and let him go'" (John 111:43-46 NIV).

"Elisha sent a messenger to say to him, 'Go, wash yourself seven times in the Jordan, and your flesh will be restored and you will be cleansed'" (2 Kings 5:10 NIV).

"So he went down and dipped himself in the Jordan seven times, as the man of God had told him, and his flesh was restored and became clean like that of a young boy" (Joel 2:25 NIV)

CHAPTER 2

BROKEN

Broken Seed

> Never underestimate the power of one tiny, broken seed. Placed in the right hands, it will surely grow into an expression of His beauty for all to see.[1]—Mary Southerland

> Very truly I tell you, unless a kernel of wheat falls to the ground and dies, it remains only a single seed. But if it dies, it produces many seeds. (John 12:24 NIV)

It is never enjoyable enduring a trial. The pain or sorrow that accompanies the struggle can be devastating and loathsome. Depression will often try to smother a weary soul, like a slow mist on a dark night.

Difficult times are permitted by God to teach us perseverance and trust, unless we have brought them on by our own sinful choices. As happened with Judas, sinning can lead to despair and hopelessness. However, reaping the consequences of our sins can result in useful spiritual lessons and gained wisdom.

There are hidden sins deep inside each of us that will only rise to the surface when we are pressed and tested. Exposed, these sins will either humble us into confessing them to God or anger us.

In the latter case, we will attempt to bury these sins once again in the depths of our very being. Thankfully, God loves us enough not to let our flaws remain hidden for long. New trials will come to bring these same sins to the surface. Until humility finds us, and our confessions are laid at the feet of Christ, the refining process will continue and address the same issues until we allow God to heal those parts of our lives.

One cannot climb a mountain before mastering specific basic skills. Sin after sin, spiritual lesson after spiritual lesson, we eventually recognize the wisdom of God's love at work in our lives. With this new maturity in Christ, we willingly allow ourselves to be broken by God's merciful hands.

It is therefore this laying down of self-will that finally propels a believer into a place of usefulness for the Lord. It is in dying that we find life. It is in serving that we obtain joy and contentment. It is by leading a selfless life that we find peace and rest for our souls.

If *we* are that single mustard seed of faith (or kernel of wheat), broken and lying on the ground, then we have the blessed opportunity to multiply for His kingdom's sake. Yes, in dying, we are watered by the hands of God—and a new harvest arises out of our single act of dying to self.

From among us broken seeds, which may be sown and transformed into plants that bear fruit, the master gardener must decide which ones He should harvest and which ones should go to seed. For, you see, the plant whose fruit is harvested is enjoyed at the banquet table of God. However, the plants permitted the honor of going to seed will either become a spice offering to God or be sown once again for an even bigger harvest the next spring.

Either way, a broken and single seed will produce much for the kingdom of God. Your trial is an opportunity to give yourself over to God. It is in dying that you will find eternal life. It is worth the breaking.

Meditate on the following three verses from Scripture.

"I planted the seed, Apollos watered it, but God has been making it grow. So neither the one who plants nor the one who waters is anything, but only God, who makes things grow" (1 Corinthians 3:6-7 NIV).

"And let us not grow weary of doing good, for in due season we will reap, if we do not give up" (Galatians 6:9 ESV).

"He who goes out weeping, bearing the seed for sowing, shall come home with shouts of joy, bringing his sheaves with him" (Psalm 126:6 ESV).

Broken, Then Reassembled

> He heals the brokenhearted and binds up their wounds. (Psalm 147:3 ESV)

> The Lord is near to the brokenhearted and saves the crushed in spirit. (Psalm 34:18 ESV)

God promises to take your broken heart and to bind up your wounds. He cannot lie, so He will faithfully keep this promise. The Great Physician will always tend to your injuries and (in His time) touch you with His healing powers. You must have faith!

There will be times when you feel like you haven't got the strength to get through another day. When you reach this point, know that you have finally broken in such a way that God can now use you. Your frame splintered, your plans destroyed, your pride laid low—God can now get to work.

He will take your broken pieces and knit them together into a thing of beauty. I say *beauty* because your final act of love, faith, and submission allows Him the creative freedom to reassemble your shards. They may not be restored in the same places as before, and you may even find that a few previously missing pieces have been located and replaced.

Rejoice. You will be whole! Your breaking gave the artist an opportunity to turn His clay into a masterpiece.

So, will you have scars? Yes, probably so, but think about a beautiful mosaic. The pieces are expertly assembled with mortar. It is made of many pieces but is still one unit, one whole. You are made of many pieces—emotions, spirit, body, mind, soul—but are still just one being. The mortar is part of the beauty in a mosaic. It is a part of the wonder. Your breaking is part of your beauty, and your spiritual scars will be badges of honor in heaven.

How God heals you will be a mystery. Since we are all so unique and different, the healing process will be uniquely designed. He has a particular healing balm for each of His children. He knows our frame and how best to approach our healing process.

For some of us, healing will come slowly and not always in a forward motion. There will be setbacks of depression, which will require our loved ones to exercise much patience. Others of us may have a bigger reserve of strength, thereby allowing God to move our healing process along at a faster rate.

When you are bruised and sore all over, remember that God is the strength of your heart. He will help you in your recovery. Never will you be alone, and never will He abandon you.

The whys and the hows may or may not be explained. We all want answers for the pain we have had to suffer, but if you really think about it, does it matter why and how? Reflection is always a good practice, but God does not have to give us answers. We can meditate on what led up to the trial, but it won't change the fact that we are in the middle of one. What *does* matter is how we react to our struggles.

Broken hearts will heal. Scars will remain. However, if we adopt a correct perspective, we may view them as beauty marks. God will see them as our crowning achievements in submission, faith, love, trust, hope, and perseverance. May He reach out today and heal all of your broken pieces.

Facing Trials: Thoughts For Meditation

The two Bible passages below are relevant to meditate on at this time:

"My flesh and my heart may fail, but God is the strength of my heart and my portion forever" (Psalm 73:27 ESV).

"Trust in the Lord with all your heart, and do not lean on your own understanding. In all your ways acknowledge Him, and He will make straight your paths" (Proverbs 3:5-6 ESV).

CHAPTER 3

PRAYER

By Hear Jesus Christ

Open the Eyes of My Heart, Lord

> I pray that the eyes of your heart may be enlightened in order that you may know the hope to which He has called you, the riches of His glorious inheritance in His holy people. (Ephesians 1:18 NIV)
>
> Indeed, we felt we had received the sentence of death. But this happened that we might not rely on ourselves but on God, who raises the dead. (2 Corinthians 1:9 NIV)

Reflection, stillness, and meditation should be a part of prayer. We need to listen for answers and instructions from God as much as we need to make petitions. When we have worries or confusion in our heart, they will eat up our energy and distract us. It takes faith to lay them down at the throne of God with an expectation that He will handle them.

Philippians 4:6 instructs us to be anxious about nothing. Through prayers and a thankful heart, we can rest in a peace that transcends all understanding. This supernatural peace is similar to that which is found in the eye of a hurricane. You will enjoy light winds and fair weather. In the eye, there is blue sky and usually no precipitation.

When a trial begins, you may be caught off guard and fall prey to the distractions and painful debris tossed your way. The whirling hurricane winds might even succeed in confusing you and thereby leave you in a daze, wondering what to do. It is not until you let go of everything you are holding onto with an iron fist and toss it back into the storm that God can finally work. He will take hold of your trouble and turn it into something amazing and wondrous.

People may think you a fool when you release troubles to God. They want you to act. They don't understand that in waiting for God to act, you are taking action. It is highly probable that they will misunderstand your act of faith and your trust in God's power. We live in a world where people fix their own problems without asking for God's help. "God helps those who help themselves" is a well-known phrase. However, it nullifies God's desire for us to rely on Him. He wants to care for us. He wants to be our provider.

Silence before God will provide you with better listening skills and improve your sensitivity to the promptings of the Holy Spirit. We are to walk by faith, not by sight. This concept will confound many of those around you, and they may call you irresponsible or a fool. But God loves to turn things into good, so any steps in faith you take will serve as a future testimony of God's faithfulness to provide for all of your needs.

God's Word will be a lamp unto your feet and will help you to find your way out of any troublesome storm. While you present your request to God, examine your heart. Ask God to reveal any sins or areas of weakness that need work. He will be faithful and will open the eyes of your heart.

These three Bible verses will help you during this time:

"The Lord is in His holy temple; let all the earth be silent before Him" (Habakkuk 2:20 NIV).

"Do not be anxious about anything, but in every situation, by prayer and petition, with thanksgiving, present your requests to God. And the peace of God, which transcends all understanding, will guard your hearts and your minds in Christ Jesus" (Philippians 4:6-7 NIV).

"Search me, God, and know my heart; test me and know my anxious thoughts. See if there is any offensive way in me, and lead me in the way everlasting" (Psalm 139:23-24 NIV).

Are Delays Denials from God?

> Then he continued, "Do not be afraid, Daniel. Since the first day that you set your mind to gain understanding and to humble yourself before your God, your words were heard, and I have come in response to them. But the prince of the Persian kingdom resisted me twenty-one days. Then Michael, one of the chief princes, came to help me, because I was detained there with the king of Persia." (Daniel 10:12-13 NIV)

God hears and answers all prayers. He will send His legion of heavenly angels, or messengers, to fulfill our prayer requests. God's angelic army is mighty and good and will always fulfill the purposes of God, but we do not battle with flesh and blood! Satan's legion is an evil, dark, and unseen army of powers and principalities with which we must fight.

When reading Daniel 10, we learn that God immediately heard Daniel's prayer. However, there was a delay in the answer to his plea. The delay was not because of God's decision to hold off and wait on things. God sent an angel to help Daniel the minute he offered the prayer. However, the heavenly angel explains that his delay was caused by a spiritual battle. The evil prince of the Persian kingdom had resisted his advancement to help Daniel for twenty-one days. It was not until the archangel Michael came to his assistance that he was able to move forward in His godly mission.

Asking for godly protection from the Evil One should be a daily part of your prayers. The Devil likes to harass and oppress the children of God. It is always a good idea to pray for a hedge of protection around you and the ones you love. Don't forget to put on the armor of Christ and keep your "sword" sharp. The Word of God is living and is sharper than any two-edged sword (Hebrews 4:12).

In Hebrews and Ephesians we are told that we can approach the throne of God with freedom and confidence. We are commanded to pray without ceasing. This means that we should be in constant communication with God throughout our day, by intercession for others and ourselves, and by giving God praise and thanks.

James 1:6 informs the believer that when he petitions God through prayer, he needs to do so without doubt. A prayer offered up in the Spirit must be offered with a confidence that God will answer it. A prayer request may not be answered in the time or way a petitioner might imagine. Do not doubt that God has heard your prayers. He listens to the cries of His children.

God has perfect timing, so you should rest in that knowledge. He has a purpose for every trial, lesson, and joyful experience you face. Each one of these events will serve to prod you along and into the fulfillment of His plans.

Jesus instructed us to be as wise as serpents and as innocent as lambs. We also need to be aware of spiritual warfare. Read and memorize the Scriptures, for they are the *living* Word and your spiritual sword. With God's Word, you can advance and attack, not just defend.

There are several reasons why you may experience a delay after offering up petitions. Perhaps your prayers are not aligned with God's plans and purpose. Or God might delay in order to keep you safe or because He has something even better planned for you. Delays could simply be the result of a spiritual battle. In all these cases, put on your armor and pray. God's angel armies are busy fighting on your behalf, and you can help by asking for God's assistance and intervention.

Meditate on these three Bible passages:

"For our struggle is not against flesh and blood, but against the rulers, against the authorities, against the powers of this dark world and against the spiritual forces of evil in the heavenly realms" (Ephesians 6:12 NIV).

"For the word of God is alive and active. Sharper than any double-edged sword, it penetrates even to dividing soul and spirit, joints and marrow; it judges the thoughts and attitudes of the heart" (Hebrews 4:12 NIV).

"Let us then approach the throne of grace with confidence, so that we may receive mercy and find grace to help us in our time of need" (Hebrews 4:16 NIV).

CHAPTER 4

OBEDIENCE

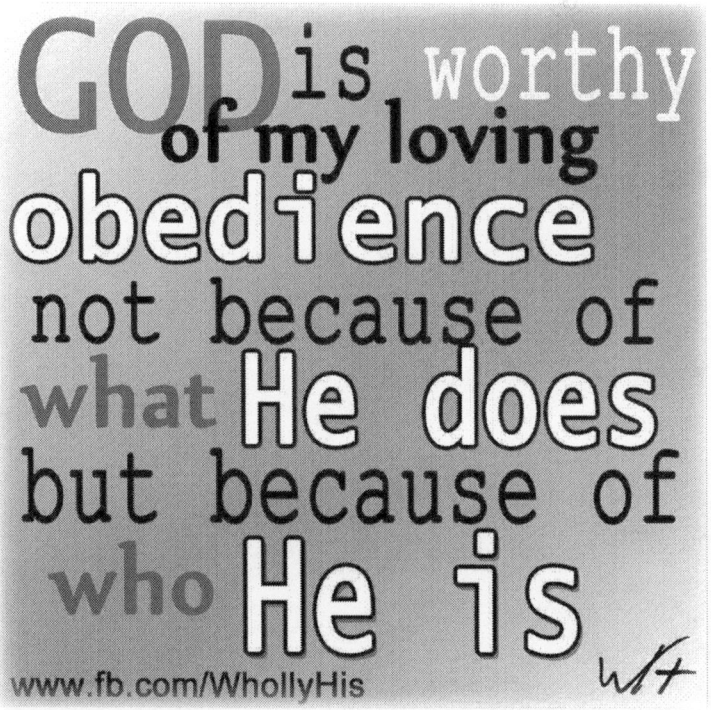

Our Obedience = Godly Results

> Rest in this—it is His business to lead, command, impel, send, call or whatever you want to call it. It is your business to obey, follow, move, respond or what have you.[1]
> —Jim Elliot

> You are my friends if you do what I command you.
> (John 15:14 ESV)

Isn't it a big weight off your shoulders to know that all God asks of you is obedience? He is the one in control and the one who will get results. All He asks of you is to obey His commandments. He will take care of the rest.

Satan fears the willing servant who prays daily these two simple words: "Use me." In 2 Timothy 2:15, Paul encourages Timothy to present himself to God as one approved, as a worker who has no cause to be ashamed. Paul stresses the importance of rightly handling the Word of Truth. If we are obedient in properly handling the Word of God, then He will do the rest.

A servant and slave must obey his or her master in *all* things, even if the request does not make sense. It is not a matter of questioning the lord of the house; it is a matter of following through on his instructions.

The Word of God tells us that if we are faithful with the little things entrusted to our care, then He will increase our responsibility and service by placing us as caretakers over much more. God tested the faithfulness, obedience, and love of Abraham and Noah. Why would he not test us in modern times?

Facing Trials: Thoughts For Meditation

If God is testing you through a personal struggle or injustice, be courageous and hold onto His promises. He is the Defender of the weak and tells His children that He will fight for them; you need only be still. *That* is a commandment, and *that* requires obedience. He will fight the battle for you and achieve the results *He* wants and requires.

Remaining still as the spiritual battle rages on around you will not be an easy thing to do, especially if you are a person of action. To be still takes self-control and faith. You are also commanded to pray without ceasing, so as you let God fight the battle before you, pray for grace and mercy. Pray that His will be accomplished and that Enemy attacks be thwarted. He and His angel armies will be shielding you and keeping you safe, as you are tucked safely under His wing.

As you obey His commands with an obedient heart, He will honor you with bigger struggles and tasks that will serve to glorify His holy name.

Consider the three quotes below:

"The Lord will fight for you; you need only to be still" (Exodus 14:14 NIV).

"His master said to him, 'Well done, good and faithful servant. You have been faithful over a little; I will set you over much. Enter into the joy of your master'" (Matthew 20:26 ESV).

"Just as a servant knows that he must first obey his master in all things, so the surrender to an implicit and unquestionable obedience must become the essential characteristic of our lives."[2]—Andrew Murray

The biblical word for *obey* comes from the Greek *hupakou*, which means "to listen attentively." The meaning also implies heeding or conforming to a command or to an authority. Basically, one has no choice in the matter whether or not to obey God's commandment. It needs to be carried out whether one agrees with the order or not.

Obedience Leads to a Future Hope

> Does it make sense to pray for guidance about the future if we are not obeying in the thing that lies before us today? How many momentous events in Scripture depended on one person's seemingly small act of obedience! Rest assured: Do what God tells you to do now, and, depend upon it, you will be shown what to do next."[3]—Elisabeth Elliot

> Does the Lord delight in burnt offerings and sacrifices as much as in obeying the Lord? To obey is better than sacrifice, and to heed is better than the fat of rams.
> (1 Samuel 15:22 NIV)

There are very deep roots in the lessons of love. Obedience is one of them. God asks us to surrender our plans and agendas to Him, so that He can conform our will to His. This means we must obediently lay down our desires, passions, hopes, and dreams. We must also lay down our loved ones at His feet. He may give them back to us just as they were, or He may alter them before returning them to us. He may adjust our hopes or change them all together. It takes faith and obedience to give them willingly over to the Father.

Fear often hinders our obedience and obscures our path to righteousness. Our Lord may ask us to do something for Him that requires a sincere and purposeful faith. Fear will often step in and try to strangle or hinder our attempt to act on God's prompt and request. This is when we need to remember the warning in Proverbs 29:25: "Fear of man will prove to be a snare, but whoever trusts in the Lord is kept safe."

Financial problems have interfered or caused many people to stumble or miss out on blessings. Worry about supporting a family can wear out any believer. However,

God may ask you to sell your house and work as a missionary in another country. The Holy Spirit may prompt you to donate money to a charity that is far beyond your budget, means, or lifestyle. Why would your God make such requests? Would He really ask you to go in an unknown and different direction? Sure, He tests our faith and obedience in many different ways. God loves when we totally rely on His provision. This means that we should rely on Him for all provisions, not just money.

There are many different trials we face in life, and through each of them, God provides for our every need. This includes strength, endurance, love, food, friends, and encouragement. He will carry us through storms. All difficulties we face with an obedient heart will turn out to be a blessing, eventually. You will see how puzzle pieces just suddenly fall into place. Your obedience—doing what He asks of you—allows Him to work wondrous things in your life. God tells us that obedience is better than sacrifice.

After you hear from God and willingly submit to His will, pray for guidance and confirmation. Be obedient to the small things in your present life and you will find your future greatly blessed, as He works out all of the details. He will surely tell you what next to do. You may not see very far into your future, but He will let you see enough of the path so you don't stumble or fall.

Be edified by these two quotes:

"Do you not know that if you continually surrender yourselves to anyone to do his will, you are the slaves of him whom you obey, whether that be to sin, which leads to death, or to obedience, which leads to righteousness" (Romans 6:16 AB).

"I find the doing of the will of God leaves me no time for disputing about His plans."[4]—George Macdonald

CHAPTER 5

OBSTACLES

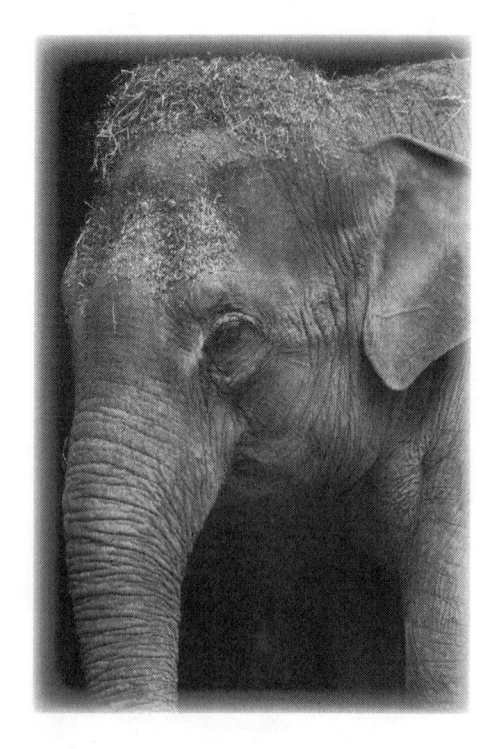

About That Elephant in the Living Room

> Cast your cares on the Lord and He will sustain you; He will never let the righteous be shaken. (Psalm 55:22 NIV)

Stop being afraid of what could go wrong, and start being positive about what could go right! God has filled the Bible with encouraging words, and He commands us *not to be afraid.* An obstacle we encounter in life will often lead us to fear. That fear will turn into anxiety and worry. Worry will then lend itself to hopelessness and depression, and then right back to fear, where it all started. Well, almost ...

I suppose the obstacle is the beginning point for fear. The trial, struggle, hardship, or mountain that God asks you to overcome can often deliver a shock to your system. You may look up to the heavens and say, "Really? Really, God?" This is when your faith and trust in His love needs to kick into gear.

He offers a peace that transcends all understanding, but we are told to go to Him in prayer and with a thankful heart in order to receive that peace. Bending a knee and falling into prayer when an obstacle is looming over our heads requires a sincere faith. The obstacle may not move, at least not for a while, but the peace could come immediately.

This promised peace must be actively claimed. It will just sit there if you do not reach out, grab it, and claim it. The choice to trust God with the matters troubling our heart is the result of our faith in His goodness and provision. Confusion, anger, and fear may destroy the peace God promises us. While it is human nature to be confused, confusion is not from God. Also, having fear and anger will delay our experiencing peace.

It is not our responsibility to fix things; God is the one in control. All a believer needs to do is submit to God, give the burden to Him, trust He will resolve the matter, and then claim the peace. This sounds easier to do than it is, since human nature is always colliding and battling things that are spiritual in nature. We will all wrestle with God at some point.

Remember that Jacob and the Virgin Mary struggled with burdens they did not wish to carry. Even the most humble and mature believer will struggle with releasing his or her burdens to the care of the Lord. However, the fact remains that the peace that *transcends all understanding* is available, and He tells us to *be anxious about nothing.*

Like an elephant in a room, the obstacle can sit. It might decide to sit for a very long time. You can watch and obsess over the problem, allowing stress to rob you of sleep. You can worry about how everything is going wrong and falling apart. Or you can stand on the promises of God and step out into life with a positive attitude. The Word tells us that all things work together for the good of those who love God and are called according to His purpose for them. So, let the elephant sit in your living room. That's fine, but get on with your life.

Like an ignored young child who is acting out for attention and then realizes he no longer has an audience, obstacles will go away. Once you have given the matter completely over to God, the obstacle will no longer be such a distraction. Satan will see that he no longer has power over you and will leave the room. There is no benefit to worry and fret. Worry only leads to evil in that it often grows into disbelief, doubt, and discouragement.

Choosing a positive outlook when faced with hardships will allow you to be a mighty witness to believers and unbelievers. The people in your life will be encouraged and amazed by the calm way in which you are walking through the fire. God may have designed the trials you face so that you have an opportunity to share God's love with someone. It takes a mature faith to say you are glad for your trials.

Therefore, "Count it pure joy when you encounter trials of many kinds, for the testing of your faith will develop perseverance" (James 1:2). This perseverance will allow you to keep your chin up. God's strength will allow you to hold onto your hope while facing the obstacles of life.

Will things always work out in the way you hoped and wanted? Of course not! You are not the illustrator of your life's painting. God has all the hues and brushstrokes worked out. The painting He is creating, thanks to the struggle He has given you, is a masterpiece. So, once again, *please stop being afraid of what could go wrong, and start being positive about what could go right.*

Pause and Consider the Words of the Scripture Below.

"And we know that God causes everything to work together for the good of those who love God and are called according to His purpose for them" (Romans 8:28 NLT).

Cheryl Zelenka

Obstacles Can Change Our Heart

> Sometimes God doesn't change your situation because He's trying to change your heart.—Unknown

> What are you, mighty mountain? Before Zerubbabel you will become level ground. Then He will bring out the capstone to shouts of, "God bless it! God bless it!"
> (Zechariah 4:7 NIV)

Jesus went before God and asked if He could escape His fate on the cross, but only if it was His Father's will. God did not have to change His Son's heart because Jesus already wanted to do His Father's bidding and trusted Him with His future.

We, on the other hand, often look at our circumstances and ask God to change them to our liking, not even considering to ask for God's will in the situation. We just want to get out of unpleasantness and strife. Obstacles alarm us, but avoiding them might not be the best thing for us.

After a personal storm, we should consider the possible lesson(s) hidden in the eye of the hurricane. We are to search ourselves and reflect. It is the mature Christian who falls to his knees when tragedy hits and asks the Lord to change his heart to accept what has been laid at his feet. The common response is to cry out, "Help!" and then, "Rescue [or deliver] me!"

But what if by leaving you in the fire, God shows you mercy *and* answers your prayers for deliverance? Sometimes God will not change your situation or remove your obstacle because He is trying to change your heart. His ways are not our ways; He holds mysteries in His hands.

Unfortunately, the human spirit is strong-willed and stubborn. It takes the trials we experience to break us of our independence. In suffering, we find ourselves repentant and dependent on Christ, which is what He longs for in His children. Do not despise the obstacles He places in your path; learn from them!

If you are walking through a difficult time, be introspective and see if you need to change your heart in some way. Maybe it is your attitude toward the length of your struggle. Could you have a hardness of heart of which you need to repent and give over to God? Do you hold onto anger, and are you shaking your fist at God for the hurdles you must overcome? Do you always ask why whenever you feel like you are a victim of some new assailant?

Stop and remind yourself of these four things:

1. God loves you with such a deep love it is beyond your ability to comprehend.
2. He honors His children with the opportunity to suffer for His name's sake.
3. The trials you suffer here on Earth are not worth comparing to the rewards and riches you will have in heaven.
4. He walks with you through every hardship. He gives you the wisdom and strength to overcome every obstacle.

Be not afraid of the trial that has been set before you. God orchestrated it before your birth, and He knows what your frame is able to withstand. Christ Himself was a bruised reed, but not a broken one. You may become bruised or be singed by the fire you must walk through, but you will never be broken or completely consumed. Like gold that is heated so that the dross can rise to the surface, the heat of your affliction is purifying you.

Put on an attitude of thanksgiving, and rejoice in your suffering. Turn your eyes upon Jesus and recall all that He suffered for your sake. Remember the saints of old and the disciples, prophets, and apostles. Let them encourage you and help you weather the challenges you face. In walking through your storm with confidence and peace, you will please your Father and win souls for Christ. May He change your heart into one of compliance and mold it into the beautiful vessel He envisioned at the beginning of time.

Below are two quotes to encourage you:

"So he [the angel] said to me, 'This is the word of the Lord to Zerubbabel: "Not by might nor by power, but by my Spirit," says the Lord Almighty'" (Zechariah 4:6 NIV).

"Pressing on in painful circumstances is the discipline of keeping our faith when everything not only goes wrong but becomes worse. It means holding onto the Lord during deep trials and asking Him to hold onto us when we feel weak in faith and hope."[1]—Sheila Cragg

CHAPTER 6

LOVE

All-Free Downloads by Vera Kratochivl

Who Are the Unlovable?

> But God demonstrates His own love for us in this: While we were still sinners, Christ died for us. (Romans 5:8 NIV)

> Do not judge by appearances, but judge with right judgment. (John 7:24 ESV)

Who are the "unlovable" in this world? How do you qualify for this very specific group of people? Is everyone in the group unlovable to everyone else in the world, or are some of the unlovable actually lovable to the rest of us?

There is nobody beyond the reach of God. He loves all of us. In fact, even while we were covered in the mud of our own sin, God sent His Son to die on the cross for us. We needed to be forgiven, and Jesus paid the price for our ransom with His blood.

Since all of us have sinned and need God's forgiveness, *all* of us have earned the "unlovable" title. Thank goodness that the love of God looks past our imperfections. Where would we be without His constant offer of love and forgiveness?

It is important to examine your heart and take an honest look at your own way of thinking regarding those you have identified as unlovable. You will probably have to admit that there are other things you consider when sending people over the fence and into the "unlovable" pasture.

Would their lack of personal hygiene be on your list of why you find certain individuals unlovable? Maybe their education, status, or profession is off-putting to you. Their physical appearance or human deformities might also be factors in your distaste.

Why is the outside appearance always the first trigger ... or is it? Do you consider greedy, pushy, loud, and boisterous folks unlovable? Does a lack of compassion or courage sweep some people you encounter into that "unlovable" category? Could a person's work ethic, or lack thereof, be irritating enough to earn them ouster from your good graces?

Even though the children of God should view people through the eyes of Jesus, many of us do not. We walk around with tinted or shaded eyeglasses that block out the goodness in people. We focus on the faults and wrongs of others, not on their accomplishments and attempts at goodness. How did Jesus see people? Did He focus on their sin, or did He love them in spite of it?

Judging is a very dangerous thing to do when you consider that we will be judged with the same measure we hand out. Jesus did not come into the world to condemn us. His purpose was always to save. Why, then, aren't we following His example?

Who are the unlovable people in your life? How have they wounded or offended you? Do they just annoy you, or do they seriously affect you when you are around them? Is your unforgiveness binding you to that "unlovable" person? Is there a plank in your own eye that needs removal, so that you can see those "unlovable" folk in your life with different eyes?

You can love any person through the grace of God. I don't mean that you have to be best friends or hang out together. Instead, why not ask God to give you His eyes the next time you run into a person you dislike? You can ask God to show you what He sees when He glances at the individual in question. This will surely give you a new perspective. It could even assist in developing compassion in your heart, along with a willingness to extend grace and mercy. You do not have to like the person, but you are commanded by God to love him or her.

Following are three Bible verses for you to meditate on:

"And the second is like it: 'Love your neighbor as yourself'" (Matthew 22:39 NIV).

"Judge not, that you be not judged. For with the judgment you pronounce you will be judged, and with the measure you use it will be measured to you" (Matthew 7:1-2 ESV).

"For God did not send his Son into the world to condemn the world, but in order that the world might be saved through Him" (John 3:17 ESV).

God Is a Gentleman

> God opens millions of flowers without forcing the buds ... reminding us not to force anything, for things happen perfectly in time.—Unknown

> He said to them: "It is not for you to know the times or dates the Father has set by His own authority." (Acts 1:7 NIV)

God is the perfect gentleman. He is always on time. In fact, His timing is impeccable. He appears just when the time is right—no sooner, no later. He is gentle, kind, respectful, loving, attentive, and in control. He has everything planned out and organized. You can trust Him to get everything done. In fact, He faithfully promises to complete the work that He has begun in you. There is no need ever to worry.

This gentleman, our God, is mighty in battle. He is a skilled warrior. Like a prince rescuing His princess, He shines in His armor as He saves you before danger has any chance of devouring you. Be not afraid! He is an awesome leader, and His angel army waits on His every word and command. He is a fierce and diligent protector.

There is no need for you to believe that your God is an apathetic listener. He longs to hear from you—not just daily, but *throughout* your day. He wants to share special moments with you as they happen. You have the freedom to talk to Him every minute of the day, even at two in the morning! You see, He never slumbers or rests. You have His undivided attention whenever you desire it!

If you are concerned about your finances, rest in the assurance that this gentleman knows how to save and give, providing for your every need. He is a Man of charity and generously gives to those in need. He believes in balanced scales and in storing up eternal treasure. He is aware of every act of kindness and each gentle witness you have performed in His name. He will give credit where credit is due.

This Lord and gentleman of ours is a master gardener and will never force things (meaning us!) to grow or bloom before their time. He waits for His fruit until it is perfectly ripened, sweet, and bountiful. He carefully tends His garden, a watering can ever at hand. He knows the perfect mix of fertilizer (organic, of course) and is careful not to use anything that would "burn" the tender shoots growing from where He so carefully planted or pruned them.

Since you are a plant in His garden, you are promised that He will never force you to do anything you don't want to do, because He honors your free choice. With love, He will daily examine you and find gentle ways to encourage growth, but He will never force your buds to bloom before they are ready.

His patience, love, and forgiving heart allow you to relax in His presence and confess wrongs that you never needed to hide. As soon as you repent, He tosses your wrongs as far as the east is from the west—and they are forgotten for eternity.

Your God is a gentleman. He will wait for you to heal and crave His attention. His desires for you are many, and He longs to see you mature and confident, lacking in nothing.

He knows how to open millions of flowers gently. He does it every day. You are one of this gentleman's most prized flowers. Your season, your time to bloom, is coming. Do not fret about when. Just know that He is a gentleman and master gardener and that you are His beloved flower. Lift your face to the Son and soak in His light. My, how beautiful His garden! How lovely are His flowers. How plentiful is His crop.

These two quotes are provided so that you may meditate on the thoughts in this chapter:

"He has made everything beautiful in its time. He has also set eternity in the human heart; yet no one can fathom what God has done from beginning to end" (Ecclesiastes 3:11 NIV).

"For the revelation awaits an appointed time; it speaks of the end and will not prove false. Though it linger, wait for it; it will certainly come and will not delay" (Habakkuk 2:3 NIV).

Chapter 7

Sin and Forgiveness

All-Free Download by John DeMers

The Potter and His Clay

> Mould us, great God, into forms of beauty and usefulness by the wheel of Providence and by the touch of Your hand. Fulfil Thine ideal, and conform us to the image of Thy Son. In Thy great house may we stand as vessels meet for Thy use. We are little better than common earthenware, but may we be cleansed, and purified, and filled with Thy heavenly treasure. Dip us deep into the River of Life, and give refreshment by us to many parched and weary hearts.[1]
> —F.B. Meyer

> This is the Word that came to Jeremiah from the Lord: "Go down to the potter's house, and there I will give you My message." So I went down to the potter's house, and I saw him working at the wheel. But the pot he was shaping from the clay was marred in his hands; so the potter formed it into another pot, shaping it as seemed best to him. Then the Word of the Lord came to me. He said, "Can I not do with you, Israel, as this potter does? Like clay in the hand of the potter, so are you in My hand, Israel." (Jeremiah 18:1-6 NIV)

God creates beautiful things. We are a wondrous creation, as we are made in the very image of Christ. Sadly, many of us look at our reflections in the mirror and cringe. We are horrified when we see who is looking back. When we focus on all our "imperfections," which I believe are determined by our culture and society, we can't see our true beauty.

The Word of God tells us that He knew us in our mother's womb. God knit us together; our frames were not hidden from Him. He imagined, formed, molded, and uniquely designed each one of us. We are the masterpieces of the one and only living God.

So why would God, our potter, need to reshape us, as Psalm 139 says that we are all fearfully and wonderfully made? The answer is sin. Our sin mars us, and our rebellion deforms us.

Thankfully, God loves His creation so much that He will not give up on us. He will never throw away the clay resting between His hands. Rather, His hands will reshape our very beings, time and time again, in order to remove our sins and rid us of our imperfections.

He may have to remold some of us several times until *we* get things right and He is satisfied with His workmanship. He does not like spiritual blemishes and will remove them in any way He sees fit. It is not creation's place to question its Creator. The number of times the potter must reshape us depends on our willingness to accept His will and the path He has laid before us. Our submission and obedience will allow the potter to work unhindered.

When God looks at you, He sees you as you *will be*. He knows of your sins, and that is why He is taking time to refashion you into something beautiful and useful. He is always looking through spiritual glasses.

If God has asked you to do something difficult, or if He is leading you into a certain ministry, check your attitude. Your path may be one full of danger and grief, but He has faithfully equipped you for your purpose. Fear and doubt will only interfere with the work He requires of you. Any hardships you face will be temporary, and they will serve a purpose.

A thankful heart should accompany you as you accept and receive His encouragements and leading. Don't turn a deaf ear to His voice. If you hesitate and ignore the prompts of the Holy Spirit,

Facing Trials: Thoughts For Meditation

watch out! Be prepared for the potter's hands making another attempt to reshape you. God's purposes will always prevail.

Take comfort in this: not only is God your potter, but He is also your Father. As a father cares for His child, so He cares for you. Patiently, He will stay by your side and work out your imperfections and blemishes.

Clay cannot mold itself. It takes the vision and the hands of One far greater to make something out of it. Clay must submit to the will of the potter. After submission is offered up as an acceptable sacrifice, trust must follow. Yes, you must trust that God is faithful to finish the work He has begun in you, and that He makes all things beautiful in His time. Trust Him. He is faithful.

Below is a Bible passages for you to meditate on:

"But who are you, O man, to talk back to God? 'Shall what is formed say to Him who formed it, "Why did You make me like this?"' Does not the potter have the right to make out of the same lump of clay some pottery for noble purposes and some for common use" (Romans 9:20-21 NIV)

Cheryl Zelenka

Nobody Is Beyond Forgiveness

> Jesus answered him, "Truly I tell you, today you will be with me in paradise." (Luke 23:43 NIV)

Jesus suffered the incredible humiliation of the cross and endured great suffering for our sake.

What does it mean that we are asked to bear the cost? It means that we must act out of forgiveness. When others commit wrongs against us, we can choose to forgive them and bear the result of what they have done. It may not be easy to bear the wrongs that others have placed on our backs, but didn't Christ do this very thing for us?

There were two criminals crucified with Christ. Both were guilty of their crimes. One of the two men mocked Jesus and threw insults His way. The other criminal acknowledged his own sin and rebuked the other criminal for his scorn toward the Redeemer.

"'Don't you fear God, since you are under the same sentence? We are punished justly, for we are getting what our deeds deserve. But this man has done nothing wrong.' He then asked Jesus to remember him upon entering His kingdom. Jesus lovingly replied, 'I tell you the truth, today you will be with me in paradise'" (Luke 23:38-43).

This act of forgiveness and hope has comforted many believers. We do not know what happens in the final moments of a person's life. This story reminds us that it is never too late to be saved and rescued from the pit of hell.

"For God so loved the world that He gave His one and only Son, that whoever believes in Him shall not perish but have eternal life" (John 3:16). Christ's is truly a wondrous love! It is a love without measure and full of grace, mercy, and hope.

While on our earthly journey, we are to walk by faith. It is by grace that we are saved, but we are also told that faith without works is dead. So, did the criminal on the cross just manage to get into heaven by the seat of his pants? Yes, probably so. Did he have any rewards or treasure laid up in heaven once he got there? Probably not. After all, he wasn't a follower and believer of Christ for very long.

How many people were at the foot of the cross witnessing this dialogue between the crucified? Some, but not thousands. Now think about this: How many people have heard this story, long after the criminal entered paradise with Jesus? More than anyone can possibly imagine.

Many people have been comforted by this story of a last-minute conversion. Wouldn't this alone earn the criminal some treasure in heaven? Could this true story be one that has led a multitude into the kingdom of God? Surely this crucified criminal has beenis given much treasure and many heavenly riches.

It is never too late to give your heart to God and start living *for* Him. If there is a lost soul you have given up on, remember that there is always hope, thanks to the blood and sacrifice of Jesus Christ. He won the battle over sin and death and died for us all, including the Prodigal Son. Because of Jesus, our sins were nailed to the cross once and for all. It is a free gift for all to receive, if only we decide to accept it. With an open heart and open arms, Jesus offers salvation to everyone. May His sacrifice and resurrection give you enough hope to pray for that "criminal" in your life.

Here, I provide you with one Bible verse to meditate on:

"Now if we died with Christ, we believe that we will also live with him. For we know that since Christ was raised from the dead, he cannot die again; death no longer has mastery over him. The death he died, he died to sin once for all; but the life he lives, he lives to God. In the same way, count yourselves dead to sin but alive to God in Christ Jesus" (Romans 6:8-11 NIV).

Chapter 8

Transformation and Refining

By Cheryl Zelenka

God Does Not Compare the Flowers in His Garden

> You don't need to be better than anyone else. You just need to be better than you used to be.—Unknown
>
> There are different kinds of gifts, but the same Spirit distributes them. There are different kinds of service, but the same Lord. There are different kinds of working, but in all of them and in everyone it is the same God at work. (1 Corinthians 12:4-6 NIV)

The refining process—which we must undergo to become what God created us to be—is a continuous one. It involves extreme pressure and, yes, pain. When God turns up the heat to melt gold, dross will rise to the surface. Dross is a collection of impurities. Sin is our impurity.

Hopefully, the refining of our spirit will bring about a forward motion in our walk with Christ. With each new lesson God sends our way, we should grow in our maturity and knowledge of Him. We are not to remain "baby" Christians all of our lives. Rather, we are meant to become mature, able to teach and witness to others.

There is danger when we start to compare our growth to the spiritual growth of others. Just as every child is different in personality and looks, so, too, is each one different in his or her abilities to learn. Growth patterns differ from individual to individual, whether we're talking about academics or spiritual lessons from our Father.

When we compare our walk to that of another, one of two things may occur. We may become convicted and then inspired to follow that person's good example, or we may become jealous and fall prey to the lies of the Enemy who jumps at any opportunity to pull down and discourage the children of God.

Just as the physical body has many parts, the body of Christ has many parts, too. Each part is dependent on the other. We need the eyes to see and the mouth to communicate. We need the hands to heal and serve and the feet to travel to far-off lands. *All* the parts are important. We can't compare the importance of body parts, because all of the parts are essential and necessary.

Look to others and be encouraged, not condemned. Map your own course of spiritual growth and monitor it to see if you are either growing in your walk or remaining in the same place. You do not want to experience stunted growth. If you see yourself as still requiring milk, like a newborn baby Christian, then take steps to stretch yourself. Allow the trials in your life to bring about your maturity. Then rejoice over the gifts allotted to your fellow brothers and sisters and be thankful for your own personal and unique talents.

A rose is beautiful, but so is an iris. Both are flowers and both are special and unique. However, they bloom in different seasons and have different aromas. They both glorify God, but in different and unparalleled ways.

That is how we are in God's eyes. We are beautiful and unique flowers in His heavenly flower garden. He adores and treasures each and every one of us.

Here, I provide you with one special Bible verse to meditate on:

> Just as a body, though one, has many parts, but all its many parts form one body, so it is with Christ. For we were all baptized by one Spirit so as to form one body—whether Jews or Gentiles, slave or free—and we were all given the one Spirit to drink. Even so, the body is not made up of one part but of many. Now if the foot should say, "Because I am not a hand, I do not belong to the body," it would not for that reason stop being part of the body. And if the ear should say, "Because I am not an eye, I do not belong to the body," it would not for that reason stop being part of the body. If the whole body were an eye, where would the sense of hearing be? If the whole body were an ear, where would the sense of smell be? But in fact God has placed the parts in the body, every one of them, just as he wanted them to be. If they were all one part, where would the body be? As it is, there are many parts, but one body. The eye cannot say to the hand, "I don't need you!" And the head cannot say to the feet, "I don't need you!" On the contrary, those parts of the body that seem to be weaker are indispensable, and the parts that we think are less honorable, we treat with special honor. And the parts that are unpresentable are treated with special modesty, while our presentable parts need no special treatment. But God has put the body together, giving greater honor to the parts that lacked it, so that there should be no division in the body, but that its parts should have equal concern for each other. If one part suffers, every part suffers with it; if one part is honored, every part rejoices with it. Now you are the body of Christ, and each one of you is a part of it. (1 Corinthians 12:12-27 NIV)

Pearls and Diamonds

> Again, the kingdom of heaven is like a merchant looking for fine pearls. When he found one of great value, he went away and sold everything he had and bought it. (Matthew 13:45-46 NIV)

You are a treasure belonging to God. He took great care in your design. Just as every snowflake, pearl, and diamond is unique, so are you! However, it takes pressure to turn a lump of coal into a diamond or a grain of sand into a pearl.

Intense pressure causes great suffering and turmoil. The transformation of our spirit as we are sanctified puts pressure on us, just as a grain of sand or would-be-diamond lump of coal is under pressure. In the end, we will be the spiritual diamond or pearl our Lord desires. However, before the Lord can press and transform us into the gem He has envisioned, we must lay down our will and submit to Him.

When you are undergoing the incredible but painful process of transformation, you will often find that the only comfort you obtain comes from the Word of God. People, even if they have good intentions, will leave you unfulfilled and empty. The Word is full of encouragement and hope. The promises of God are many and should be read during times of weakness and doubt, struggle and hardship.

No soul, pearl, or diamond will remain in the dark ocean or earth forever. Something will come along to propel it to the surface. You will be discovered, admired, loved, and treasured by the ones who find you. The almighty God already knows about your beauty; here, I am speaking about those around you who finally discover your value as you live out His purpose for your life.

You are the pearl in Matthew 13:45-46. God is the merchant. When finding you, He sees your value and sells everything He has in order to purchase you. Jesus purchased you with His blood. You are His treasure. Think about your value and your cost to God. With this in mind, can you now endure the sanctification process?

Meditate on the words of this scripture.

"Submit to God and be at peace with Him; in this way prosperity will come to you" (Job 22:21 NIV).

Chapter 9

Endurance and Perseverance

Tree by Cheryl Zelenka

Don't Give Up!

> Battles are fought in our minds every day. When we begin to feel the battle is just too difficult and want to give up, we must choose to resist negative thoughts and be determined to rise above our problems. We must decide that we're not going to quit. When we're bombarded with doubts and fears, we must take a stand and say: "I'll never give up! God's on my side. He loves me, and He's helping me! I'm going to make it!"[1]—Joyce Meyer

> May you be strengthened with all power, according to His glorious might, for all endurance and patience with joy, giving thanks to the Father, who has qualified you to share in the inheritance of the saints in light. (Colossians 1:11-12 NIV)

Perseverance with faith enables a person to overcome the greatest of difficulties. A committed faith in God's provision and protection will give you the endurance necessary to persevere amid even the most challenging of circumstances. Without perseverance, it is impossible to finish the race God has asked you to run. He wants all of His children to make it past the finish line, so don't let any snare from the Enemy deceive and deter you. Take all thoughts captive and ask the Holy Spirit to help you in discerning the discouraging lies of the Enemy.

It is through trials, hardships, tests, and storms that we gain our spiritual endurance. Sadly, many Christians are unable to maintain the necessary endurance to see Christ faithfully bring their trial to its rightful conclusion. Perseverance requires a believer to stand on a faith that trusts in God's goodness and love. He will provide you with a supernatural strength to see you through every problem you face. However, you must maintain your hope and patiently wait out any storm or trial He permits.

If you try to persevere through a struggle with only self-reliance and on your own strength alone, you will not make it through without suffering an injury or completely failing. God warns us not to "live in [our] own light and warm [ourselves] by [our] own fires" (Isaiah 50:11 ESV). Persevering includes being still and letting God fight for you. Patience accompanies perseverance, endurance, and faith.

Also, remember that miracles happen today. You may even be blessed to witness one firsthand. Maybe *you are* the miracle. God can heal people for His glory, bringing new believers into His fold.

It is very possible that God will use your personal trial to spur other believers on in their walk. God wants us to comfort other weary souls with the comfort we have experienced through Him. If we don't persevere in facing a storm, we could be setting a ripple effect into action and miss blessings from God. All opportunities to serve are blessings.

In addition, God is the same then, now, and in the future. He performed many miracles in the times before and after Jesus walked the earth as the Son of Man. He still performs miracles today, and He uses some of His faithful servants to heal and restore in miraculous ways. It requires perseverance to identify the gifts He has given us and to practice them for His purposes. Stepping out and doing His work requires a persevering faith.

If you are weary and feel like you just can't go another step, please don't quit. Our path is uphill to keep us from going down to the grave. An uphill climb requires strength and perseverance to eventually reach the summit of God. You can climb any mountain with God who strengthens you.

Meditate on these three quotes:

"The path of life leads upward for the wise, that he may keep away from Sheol below" (Proverbs 15:24 NASB).

"But watch out, you who live in your own light and warm yourselves by your own fires. This is the reward you will receive from me: You will soon fall down in great torment" (Isaiah 50:11 NLT).

"To learn strong faith is to endure great trials. I have learned my faith by standing firm amid severe testings."[2]—George Mueller

It Takes Endurance to Scale a Mountain of God

For though the righteous fall seven times, they rise again, but the wicked stumble when calamity strikes. (Proverbs 24:16 NIV)

During your Christian walk, you will encounter many challenges and lessons. The Lord understands your limitations, but He *will* send challenging opportunities for spiritual growth your way. These trials and lessons will stretch your abilities. After all, if your lessons were only about things you have already mastered, then how would you grow?

God does not expect us to perfect all of His lessons the first time we encounter them. Schools will often use a curriculum that builds on concepts taught in previous years. They call this a "spiral curriculum." Students at one grade level may be introduced to a concept, while students at a higher grade level will revisit and review the original concept and then receive additional information which is provided to challenge the student. In this way, the student's knowledge of the concept builds over a period of years.

The Father will take a similar approach when teaching His children important spiritual lessons. For example, as children, we are introduced to the concept of love. If you were lucky, you grew up in a home with loving parents and extended family members. You knew security and felt safe. In your early years, you probably received love more than you gave it. As you grew in years, your lessons in love took on new aspects. You may have been introduced to the concept of giving out of a pure heart. Developing unconditional love is a lesson reserved for more mature believers. God usually does not start us out in this spiritual college-level course.

As God sends a lesson your way, whether it is one of hardship or of joy, be diligent in learning all that He intends for you to grasp. You may fall, but Proverbs 24:16 (NIV) states, "The righteous fall seven times, only to rise again." Perseverance requires us to be steadfast and patient. Endurance is a prerequisite of perseverance. You cannot move forward in your spiritual journey unless you put one foot in front of the other! It takes strength to walk or run, and it takes perseverance to continue forward to your destination.

Scaling a mountain requires physical strength, endurance, and perseverance. If you look at the whole ascent while at the base, you may easily become overwhelmed. Mountaineers will break down and plan their ascent, often on a day-by-day basis, since weather can cause all kinds of problems. In a similar manner, God breaks down lessons and tasks for us. He does not want us to be anxious or overwhelmed.

When approaching a mountainous climb, the first goal is to get the proper climbing equipment. In a spiritual climb, this means dressing yourself in the armor of Christ. Then look into maps and into finding a guide. In a spiritual sense, this means equipping yourself by reading God's instruction manual and praying that He His will be your guide. The ascent to the "base camp" will be the next step. Every night a new plan is made in order to reach the next mountainous destination, until the summit is finally reached.

The lessons God sends your way are meant to be for your benefit. They are sent with love. He prepares you for that which He created you to perform for His glory. He will not send a soldier into battle without armor, nor will He send His child down a dark path without a light.

Facing Trials: Thoughts For Meditation

May you accept your lessons in life with an obedient heart and a desire to please the Holy One. They will stretch and mold you into the masterpiece He knows you already are, once His glory is revealed. Climb with the confidence and endurance of a deer jumping from mountain cliff to mountaintop.

Pause and meditate on the words taken from the book of Habakkuk.

"The Sovereign Lord is my strength; He makes my feet like the feet of a deer, He enables me to tread on the heights" (Habakkuk 3:19 NIV).

Chapter 10

Spiritual Path and Spiritual Journey

Life in a Fog

> For now we see only a reflection as in a mirror; then we shall see face to face. Now I know in part; then I shall know fully, even as I am fully known. (1 Corinthians 13:12 NIV)

> Your word is a lamp for my feet, a light on my path. (Psalm 119:105 NIV)

Do you ever feel like you are living your life in a fog? Has your vision for the future been impaired or somehow veiled? Are you looking at a fuzzy world, as if there is still sleep in your eyes?

The Word of God tells us that while we work out our salvation on Earth, we will only see part of the whole picture God has designed for us. This means that we have only pieces of the puzzle, and they are barely visible through the fog. This includes what we know and understand of the heavenly realm. Right now, we have only a poor idea of what heaven will be like, not to mention our Creator. We can't comprehend the full riches and glory that will be revealed to us upon entering our eternal home.

God holds many mysteries in His hand. He reveals only portions of them to us and then requires us to walk with Him in faith. In fact, our futures are dictated by faith—*blind* faith. To our eyes, the path may often appear fuzzy, but to the eyes of God, it is always perfectly clear which direction He must take us. He knows who we will become, where our ministries will lie, and to which valley, desert, or mountaintop He must lead us.

It is highly probable that the "fog" God provides is for your benefit. If you were to see too far into your future, you would become overwhelmed. Imagine if God told you, when you were a child, that you would suffer a brain tumor and nearly die? What if He showed you the death of a brother or a personal sin that caused the death of an innocent person? How would you bear it? He knows your frame; He knows that you are but dust. He carries the burdens of the world on His shoulders so that you can concentrate on living just one day at a time.

When thick fog allows for only limited vision, you will be able to see just far enough ahead to safely place one foot in front of the other. This concept parallels the portions of the Sermon on the Mount that exhort us not to worry about tomorrow because each day has enough cares to keep us occupied. When we look too far ahead into the future, we become overburdened. God will help us carry the load on our backs, as He wants us to be effective witnesses for Him.

If your trial has left you confused or wondering why things have turned out as they have, then pray. God will always talk to His children. He may not give answers to all of your questions (for your own good), but He will send you encouragement and words of hope and love.

To trust Him with your uncertain future is to love Him with your whole heart.

These two quotes are for you to consider in light of the above:

"Therefore do not worry about tomorrow, for tomorrow will worry about itself. Each day has enough trouble of its own" (Matthew 6:34 NIV).

"God has wisely kept us in the dark concerning future events and reserved for himself the knowledge of them, that he may train us up in a dependence upon himself and a continued readiness for every event."[1]—Matthew Henry

Looking Back Old Chapters vs. New Chapters

> "*You can't start the next chapter of your life if you keep re*-reading your last one."[2]—Nancy Holowaty

> The righteous keep moving forward, and those with clean hands become stronger and stronger. (Job 17:9 NLT)

Forget the former things; do not dwell on the past. See, I am doing a new thing! Now it springs up; do you not perceive it? I am making a way in the wilderness and streams in the wasteland. (Isaiah 43:18-19 NIV)

If you carry around regrets and sorrows that keep your focus on the past, you might be missing your present and future blessings. You will not have your eyes on the favor God is trying to hand you on a daily basis. If your eyes are always looking backwards, you are blind to the things before you. You really do not want to miss out on any of the Lord's blessings.

For those bent on constantly looking back, you are in great peril of falling, or at least of stumbling on your path. When your eyes are not facing forward and you are gazing at things long past, how can you possibly see the dangers in front of you?

Think of the posture you would have to assume in walking forward, with your neck turned and your eyes looking at the road you have already traveled. To say that this is awkward and clumsy is an understatement.

Now imagine a person with his eyes looking back while he is attempting to climb a mountain. He would not get very far, indeed! His hands would feel for handholds and would surely find them at first, but there will come a time when handholds are few and far between. At these moments, you need your eyes looking forward and searching for those hidden places that you can grasp. They are necessary if you want to get a solid footing once again.

Grief over events that have already transpired is one of the things that keeps us focused on the past. It is like a cloaked hood. When it is worn over the head of a believer, it succeeds in hiding sorrow from those who would willingly share it and carry it a mile or two. The hood keeps others out, but it also keeps you in. You become a prisoner of sorts. A hooded cloak of grief impairs your vision and blocks all the goodness around you. You can become imprisoned by memories, good though they may be. Memories are to be stored up and treasured, for certain, but they are not to be used as an excuse to stop living your life for Christ.

If your spouse has died and gone to heaven, he or she is waiting for you. The two of you were made as one person. Your spirits can't be separated. This is part of the miracle found in a marriage union. But do consider this: Would your dearly departed loved one want you to live the rest of your years on Earth in the past, with only memories to hold? Would he or she encourage you to build new memories, even if he or she is not in them? Maybe your new memories will be shared with your loved one, once you are finally reunited in God's kingdom.

Choosing to look ahead and focus on what is before you is not an act of betrayal to the one you love. God wants to do new things in your life. He is a *lifelong teacher,* and you, in turn, should strive to be a *lifelong learner.* He wants you to accomplish all that He has planned for you to do. He promises to make a way for you to fulfill His purposes. He will refresh you and heal your wounds when you are just too tired to move another step ... so long as you do eventually get up and move along.

God does not want us to be a backward-looking people, going through life missing all the blessings He has for us along the way to glory. Ask yourself this: Are you ready to start the next chapter of your life, or are you going to reread the last one over and over again?

Keep in mind these two quotes:

"But Lot's wife looked back, and she became a pillar of salt" (Genesis 19:26 NIV).

"Beware of looking back at what you once were, when God wants you to become someone you've never been."[3]
—Oswald Chambers

CHAPTER 11

FEAR

> "I tell you, my friends, do not be afraid of those who kill the body and after that can do no more. But I will show you whom you should fear: Fear him who, after the killing of the body, has power to throw you into hell. Yes, I tell you, fear him."
> Luke 12:4-5

By Hear Jesus Christ

Fear Cripples and Trips Up the Believer

> For God did not give us a spirit of timidity [fear], but a spirit of power, of love and of self-discipline. (2 Timothy 1:7 NIV)

> Fear of man will prove to be a snare, but whoever trusts in the Lord is kept safe. (Proverbs 29:25 NIV)

We are told that God did not give us a spirit of timidity or fear. Rather, He gave us a spirit of *power*. This power that comes from God is full of His wisdom and strength.

The key ingredient of His godly power in us is *love*. Love is a mighty weapon. In 1 Corinthians 13:13, it is called "the greatest gift of all." Why, then, is love even greater than faith and hope?

When you love your enemies with the love of God, you startle them into a state of reflection. They will become confused as they ponder their hateful actions and the contradictory response of your love and kindness. They will be stumped.

Confusion is, of course, a tool of the Devil, so you will need to pray that God reveal the truth to the "enemy" you are trying to love. Ultimately, our earthly purpose is to win souls to Christ.

If you do not see a change in the other person's behavior, it does not mean that you haven't planted a seed. God has the watering can and will water that which you have planted in His name. He is always faithful to complete the work that has begun in you and others. Continue to pray that the scales over the eyes of your "enemy" fall away. Ask God to open the eyes of that person's heart so that he or she may receive the truth. Pray for a hedge of protection around the person so that the fiery darts of the Evil One are rendered powerless. As Christ intercedes on your behalf, you need to intercede on the other person's behalf.

The strength and power you have received from God also contains self-discipline. This means that you have the power to turn an offense into an act of love. It takes self-control to withhold vengeance and retribution or to control a quick tongue. If you respond to an unkind act as most in the world might, then you will lose an opportunity to shine the love of God onto a situation. It is at such moments that you must call on the *power* of the Holy Spirit.

God commanded Joshua "to be strong and courageous." He added, "Do not be terrified or discouraged." This directive is hard for human beings to follow, especially when we face foes the size of giants. Joshua was encouraged when God said He would be with him wherever he went. This promise applies to us as well. We do not need to be terrified when enemies approach us, as God is always standing right beside us. When we return an unkind act with one of love, we should not become discouraged if we do not witness a sudden change in the individual. Change may happen on the inside of his or her heart, where only God can observe and care for it.

Fear is a snare the Enemy uses to hinder the work of God. Proverbs 29:25 warns us about fearing humankind. By trusting in God, we are always kept safe. If we are led to speak or minister to a person in power, we should not let his or her position stop us from doing what the Lord asks of us. By trusting in His power, we will be kept safe. He is not a respecter of persons or positions. He is the one who gave us our position and power in the first place. It was His to hand out.

Remember, the Enemy uses fear to hinder our accomplishing what God has asked of us. We have been *commanded* by God to remain courageous and not become discouraged. Love is a mighty tool, and all believers should be using it to win their "enemies" to Christ. It is the Devil who trembles at the mere mention of the name of Jesus. With God's power, we are equipped with self-control, which enables us to respond to hateful acts with love. Acts of love performed in the name of Christ will always put fear into the Devil's own heart.

Do you love your neighbors as yourself? Why not extend the love of Christ to everyone around you today, and pray for your enemies? Do not let hardship, grief, or pain hinder God's command to you to love with His supernatural love. His love is planted deep inside you and wants to bear fruit. Just be sure to remember to water that which you have sown and check on its growth every once in a while.

In your meditation, reflect on these three Bible verses:

"But here is what I tell you. Love your enemies. Pray for those who hurt you. Then you will be sons of your Father who is in heaven" (Matthew 5:44-45 NIV).

"Have I not commanded you? Be strong and courageous. Do not be terrified; do not be discouraged, for the Lord your God will be with you wherever you go" (Joshua 1:9 NIV).

"And now these three remain: faith, hope and love. But the greatest of these is love" (1 Corinthians 13:13 NIV).

Fear Is a Prison

> For God has not given us a spirit of fear and timidity, but of power, love, and self-discipline. (2 Timothy 1:7 NLT)

> There is no fear in love. But perfect love drives out fear, because fear has to do with punishment. The one who fears is not made perfect in love. (1 John 4:18 NIV)

Fear is a trap that leads us to prison. Emotionally speaking, fear can strangle the hope and life out of a person. It will not hesitate to cripple, wound, or harass a believer. Fear loves to cast doubt and disturb the peace in our soul. It destroys love and has the ability to paralyze the children of God. Fear is a bully. Fear is the Devil in disguise.

First John 4:18 tells us that there is no fear in love. God has a perfect love for us, and it is able to drive out all fear. We must strive to attain that perfect love of God and remember that He is not looking to punish us. If anything, God loves us so much that He wants to instruct and discipline us with His mercy and grace.

If you are facing a struggle that intimidates you or causes you fear, take comfort in Joshua 1:9. In this verse, you are *commanded* to be courageous. In addition, you are instructed not to be afraid or discouraged. There is also a promise in this Scripture. The Lord says He will be with you wherever you go. This means that God will walk with you through sorrow, pain, and change, and through journeys into the desert or valley. He will also walk beside you as you climb to the mountaintops. You need not fear because the most powerful being is right beside you.

There will be moments in your walk when you feel so passionately for Christ and are so effective at serving Him that the Enemy will notice you and balk. He will then most likely get angry and try to sabotage your service or ministry. This is when you need to remember that the angel of the Lord encamps around those who fear Him, and that the Lord also delivers them from fear.

Psalm 91:4-8 reminds us that He will shield us with His wings and that His faithful promises are our armor of protection. The promises of God are in the Bible. His promises are a part of His living Word. The Word of God is the sword with which we must battle principalities and powers of darkness.

What are some of the *promises* of God you should memorize and hold claim to, especially at times when you are under spiritual attack? Jeremiah 29:11 promises that He has plans to prosper you with a hope and a future. Matthew 11:28 promises to give rest to the weary. Isaiah 40:29 promises to give strength to the weary. Philippians 4:19 assures believers that all needs will be supplied.

Fear lives in every heart, but it does not have to rule the heart. When the cares of this world cause you to fear or inspire feelings of being overwhelmed, cast them up to your Savior. Allow Him to shelter you in the shadow of His wings and give you peace and rest.

Allow the three Bible quotes below to guide your meditation:

"The angel of the Lord encamps around those who fear Him, and He delivers them" (Psalm 34:7 NIV).

"This is My command—be strong and courageous! Do not be afraid or discouraged. For the Lord your God is with you wherever you go" (Joshua 1:9 NLT).

"He will cover you with His feathers. He will shelter you with His wings. His faithful promises are your armor and protection. Do not be afraid of the terrors of the night, nor the arrow that flies in the day. Do not dread the disease that stalks in darkness, nor the disaster that strikes at midday. Though a thousand fall at your side, though ten thousand are dying around you, these evils will not touch you" (Psalm 91:4-8 NLT).

CHAPTER 12

FAITH

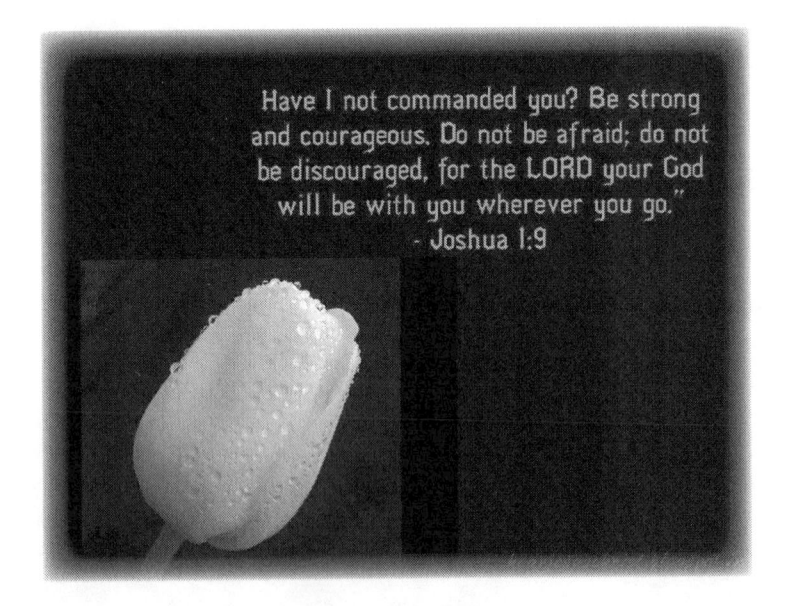

> Have I not commanded you? Be strong and courageous. Do not be afraid; do not be discouraged, for the LORD your God will be with you wherever you go."
> - Joshua 1:9

By Hear Jesus Christ

Shipwrecked and Broken, But Safe

> Now faith is confidence in what we hope for and assurance about what we do not see. (Hebrews 11:1 NIV)

Paul was placed on a ship so that he could make an appeal to Caesar. On his ocean voyage, he encountered a nor'easter (Acts 27:14). This is a storm with the wind force of a hurricane. For three days, sailors battled the storm, throwing overboard cargo and the ship's tackle. Then, "When neither sun nor stars appeared for many days and the storm continued raging, [they] finally gave up all hope of being saved" (Acts 27:20).

An angel of the Lord appeared to Paul and told him not to be afraid. Paul would not drown because it was God's will for him to stand trial before Caesar. It was not time for Paul to embark on his journey to his eternal home. God had more plans for him to fulfill on Earth. The angel then told Paul, "God has graciously given you the lives of all who sail with you."

Paul shared this news with the crew and encouraged them to keep up their courage. Paul's faith allowed him to support and embolden everyone on board, even those who were his captors. On the fourteenth stormy night, the ship hit a sandbar. Those on board were able to swim to shore and all lives were saved, just as the angel had foretold.

There may be incredibly dark storms in your life right now or on the horizon, but if your eyes are on His will and not your circumstances, you will survive the storm. Faith must carry you through your trial. God will not let the Enemy snatch you out of the palm of His hand before He is finished with you. He has a purpose for your life.

Paul accepted the angel messenger's word of safety in faith. In turn, he encouraged and instructed those on the ship with him. Those on board witnessed Paul's calm confidence and followed his instructions when they themselves were overcome with fear. The confidence of the Lord is our strength, as it was Paul's strength when he faced the possibility of a shipwreck.

It takes faith to jump into uncertain waters, especially if you don't know how to swim. Faith will enable you to find that unseen floating log to hold onto, or God will give you the strength and skills to make it to safety. His pathway for your life holds valuable lessons and a mighty purpose for you. Don't let fear weaken your faith and lead you to "go down with the ship."

The Christian walk is a walk of faith, not emotion. We can't make decisions based on what feels good. The Bible promises us not only blessings, but troubles as well. Our faith will be tested as we face many uncomfortable situations. However, these tests are for our benefit. They will strengthen our determination to rely on God. They will also build our confidence in God's promise to walk with us every step of the way, during good times and bad.

A Christian walk requires a believer to remember God's goodness, love, and promises. Your life might have to break apart like the ship Paul was on, but God will bring you to safety and dry land. He will rebuild your life, making it even better than before. He created you, so He knows how to reassemble you.

These three Scriptures are provided so that you may reflect on them in your meditations:

Facing Trials: Thoughts For Meditation

"I have told you these things, so that in Me you may have peace. In this world you will have trouble. But take heart! I have overcome the world" (John 16:33 NIV).

"For the Lord will be at your side and will keep your foot from being snared" (Proverbs 3:21 NIV).

"I give them eternal life, and they shall never perish; no one will snatch them out of My hand" (John 10:28 NIV).

Keep Your Eyes on Jesus

> Look into My eyes and you'll find Me. Look into My heart and you'll find you.—Anonymous
>
> "Lord, if it's You," Peter replied, "tell me to come to You on the water." "Come," He said. Then Peter got down out of the boat, walked on the water and came toward Jesus. But when he saw the wind, he was afraid and, beginning to sink, cried out, "Lord, save me!" Immediately Jesus reached out His hand and caught him. "You of little faith," He said, "why did you doubt?" (Matthew 14:28-31)

Have you ever wondered why the story of Peter's attempt to walk on water made it into the Bible? Our Creator has selected each word and every story for His blessed instruction manual. He teaches us, as well as warns and encourages us, throughout every page of His Word.

Peter had enough faith to cry out to Jesus and to get out of the boat. That latter act alone took a great measure of faith and courage. There were a few moments when Peter actually walked on the water to Christ. Sadly, when the furious winds of the storm distracted him, fear entered his heart and he began to sink. With his eyes off Christ, his circumstances and surroundings overwhelmed him and his faith faltered.

Jesus reached out to Peter when he cried, "Lord, save me!" Our Lord will *always* reach out for His children when we ask to be saved. His compassion is endless. However, upon reaching the boat, Jesus rebuked Peter for his lack of faith. Peter's doubt that Christ would keep him safe was Peter's undoing. Anytime we lose sight of God, we will forget from where our help comes.

Nothing is impossible with Christ, so circumstances are not going to interfere with His care for you.

Reflect a minute and ask yourself if there are any circumstances in your life causing you to be fearful. Have you taken your eyes off God? Did you start out like Peter, trusting Him to take care of you? Did you walk for some time in your personal storm with Christ? Were you surprised and amazed by the progress you were making during such a challenging and dangerous journey? How long were your eyes fixed on Jesus and not on the swirling waves around you? Why did your eyes leave the reassuring glance and love of your Master? What made you look away?

Say you are in a storm right now. Let this Bible story encourage, instruct, guide, and possibly rebuke you. Do not be like Peter. Keep your eyes fixed on your Savior, not on your circumstances. Your Lord will see you through the toughest and scariest of storms. You have a purpose. He has a plan for you. Let the storm serve to deepen your faith, and do not doubt that He holds you in the palm of His hand. He is your strength and your shield. Let the storms come, for you have nothing to fear. Just keep looking into His loving eyes and you will confidently weather your storm.

If you have taken your eyes off Christ and you feel yourself slipping into the sea of despair, cry out to the Lord. Just as Jesus saved Peter from a watery grave, He will save you. God had more plans for Peter, so his death was not even an option that stormy night. He has plans for you, too. Put your focus back on Christ and pray. You will find yourself placed back in the safety of your boat, and He will calm your storm with these two simple words: "Be still."

Following are two Bible verses for your consideration:

"Fixing our eyes on Jesus, the Pioneer and Perfecter of faith. For the joy set before Him He endured the cross, scorning its shame, and sat down at the right hand of the throne of God" (Hebrews 12:2 NIV).

"But Jesus looked at them and said, 'With man this is impossible, but with God all things are possible'" (Matthew 19:26 EVS).

CHAPTER 13

FREE WILL AND GOD'S WILL?

All-Free Downloads by Brainsman

God's Will and His Willingness

> Heal me, Lord, and I will be healed; save me and I will be saved, for You are the one I praise. (Jeremiah 17:14 NIV)

God can do all things. He is the great I Am, the giver of life, and the Creator of the universe. He is almighty in power and a just God. So why does He heal some and not others? A look into the words *willing* and *will* may shed some light.

I define *willing* as "having a specific attitude in which one is inclined to grant something." This would include a tendency to lean in favor of something proposed. I define *will* as "an intention, purpose, or desire."

When Jesus was in the garden of Gethsemane praying to His Father, He asked God if it were possible to avoid the crucifixion. Jesus then submitted to God by saying, "Yet not My will, but what You will." Jesus was asking God if He was *willing,* or *inclined,* to find a different means whereby to ransom the people of the world as adopted children of God.

God's response to Jesus was a silent no. Jesus had to face the cross and carry the sins of the world on His back. The death of the Father's beloved Son was the means to a greater end. The crucifixion was God's plan, and His purposes are always completed. We may not understand how things work for good or why they must be, but through faith we grow to accept His plans and purpose as perfect and just.

It was God's *will,* or *intention,* to sacrifice His own Son so that all believers could live an eternal life through the blood of Jesus. Was this an easy or joyful decision for Jesus or God the Father?

No, but Jesus *willingly* became the sacrificial lamb and agreed to the *will* of God, for He trusted His Father and knew His plan was perfect.

Let us now return to the question of why God heals some and not others. There is most certainly a greater goal to be accomplished by a person's illness or sudden or premature death. A serious illness could cause someone to earnestly consider his or her eternal destiny and come to knowledge of Christ. Sadly, a death may be the only thing that gets someone's attention. Through sorrow, we often examine our life and the condition of our own heart.

Therefore, what the Enemy intends as evil, God can always turn into a greater good. God's intentions, desires, and *will* are to have us draw near to Him. If it takes a tragedy or even an early and unexpected death to draw us near to God, then we must accept that event as the *will* of God. Yes, we must trust that His intentions far outweigh what we are *inclined* to pray for when we seek our God's favor.

We can be comforted in knowing that God is in control and that He has a loving purpose or plan, a plan to prosper and not harm us. When tragedy strikes, we can fail to see or understand the good in the situation. Pain, loss, fear, and anger may be all we can feel and conceive of. To find the potential prosperity in tragic events requires soul-searching, but it is made easier when we fully understand that God is not out to harm and destroy His beloved children. During these very difficult times, our "walking by faith" will rescue us from the pit of despair dug by the Enemy, who will always try to create hopelessness out of difficult circumstances. Jeremiah 29:11 tells us that God's plans for all of His children include "a plan with a hope and a future."

Even if that future is with a sick loved one who faces an early death, we must by faith choose to recognize that "in all things God works for the good of those who love him, who have been called according to His purpose" (Romans 8:28 NIV). Who knows how many souls will be won for Christ through the loss of the one you care for with such devotion?

Is your spiritual walk one where you accept the will of God in your life with little or no question? Are you *willing* to accept His plan for you and His purpose for those near you, no matter the cost? Can you lay down your will and desires for His sake? His purpose is always just. God does not have to explain His plan to His creation. Sometimes He will, but usually we are required to trust in His love for us and submit to His will. Walking by faith means that we trust in the purposes of God even when we don't understand them.

The two passages below are for your personal reflection:

"They went to a place called Gethsemane, and Jesus said to His disciples, 'Sit here while I pray.' He took Peter, James and John along with Him, and He began to be deeply distressed and troubled. 'My soul is overwhelmed with sorrow to the point of death,' He said to them. 'Stay here and keep watch.' Going a little farther, He fell to the ground and prayed that if possible the hour might pass from Him. 'Abba, Father,' He said, 'Everything is possible for You. Take this cup from Me. Yet not what I will, but what You will'" (Matthew 26:32-36 NIV).

"For God so loved the world that He gave His one and only Son, that whoever believes in Him shall not perish but have eternal life" (John 3:16).

Stumbles, Skinned Knees, and Open Arms

> If we only have the will to walk, then God is pleased with our stumbles.[1]—C.S. Lewis

> When he came to his senses, he said, "How many of my father's hired servants have food to spare, and here I am starving to death! I will set out and go back to my father and say to him: 'Father, I have sinned against heaven and against you. I am no longer worthy to be called your son; make me like one of your hired servants.'" So he got up and went to his father. But while he was still a long way off, his father saw him and was filled with compassion for him; he ran to his son, threw his arms around him and kissed him. (Luke 15:17-20 NIV)

Free will is one of God's many gifts to His children. He made us with His powerful love, and He wants our love in return. But He will never force us to reciprocate His love. If He ordered us to love Him, without the option of free choice, then our love offering would not be a true and pure one.

When we choose to love God, laying our will at His feet is part of the sacrificial offering. Love is never self-seeking, so our will must fall to the ground. A committed believer will choose to hand over the heart God created and say, "It is Yours to do with as You will."

In Deuteronomy 30, we learn that with free will there is life and prosperity, death and destruction. We are commanded to love and obey God by keeping His commandments. He wants us to choose life, but always the gift of free will remains to choose death instead.

When you acknowledge that your heart belongs to the Creator, walking with Him will be your greatest desire. And, just as a toddler when learning to walk, you will stumble and fall. This is part of the learning process. God understands. He is pleased with your decision to walk with Him, and He has no objection to your holding onto His hand to avoid stumbling.

However, when and if you stumble, you can be sure that God will accept you back with open arms. Think of the Prodigal Son. He finally humbled himself and went back home to his father. Surprised by his overwhelming, loving welcome home, that son would remain faithful and loyal to his father—with gratitude in his heart—forever.

When we follow the wayward path of the Prodigal Son, only faith and humility will bring us back home to Father God. The love of the Father will keep us by His side as we hold tightly to His gift of forgiveness. We will continue to stumble, but God will smile as we seek to pick ourselves up and choose to take the hand He offers. He does not look at our failures; rather, He sees our growth. He sees the positives and our attempts to grow in goodness, not the wrongs and sins the Devil highlights and wishes to use as evidence for why we should be condemned.

Difficult times may be the catalyst used to propel your return to an active life with Christ. The hardships you experience could be the actual hand of God reaching down from heaven to save you.

The nail-pierced hands of His Son are all you need to remember if you begin to question God's love for you. Choose to accept His hand, and let Him lead you. His grace will be sufficient to carry you on your way to glory. You may skin your knees many more times along the way, but God carries an endless supply of Band-Aids to patch you up. Since you will stumble, I recommend a good pair of spiritual hiking boots. And by the way, the armor of Christ *does* include "sandals of peace."

Take time to reflect upon the following scripture.

"See, I set before you today life and prosperity, death and destruction. For I command you today to love the Lord your God, to walk in obedience to Him, and to keep His commands, decrees and laws; then you will live and increase, and the Lord your God will bless you in the land you are entering to possess" (Deuteronomy 30:15-16 NIV).

CHAPTER 14

HEALING

All-Free Downloads by George Hodan

"I'm Cracked, Lord, and I Need Healing!"

> There is a crack in all things. This is how the light of God enters to heal and instruct.[1]—Cheryl Zelenka

> Truly, truly, I say to you, unless a grain of wheat falls into the earth and dies, it remains alone; but if it dies, it bears much fruit. (John 12:24 ESV)

> The Lord is close to the brokenhearted and saves those who are crushed in spirit. (Psalm 34:18 NIV)

When you have a broken heart, the crack itself will allow the healing power of God to enter, transform, advise, and heal it. You will never be crushed beyond repair. The Great Physician will bind up your wounds and bring about your miraculous healing, in His time. A broken bone takes time to heal; so does a broken heart or spirit.

Everyone in this world experiences trials, grief, and hardships. This is a reality of life from which no one is excluded. God sends struggles our way so that we may build our relationship with Him and so that He may get our attention, teach us lessons, and help us develop perseverance. With free will, we have a choice to lean on Him during these times, or we may attempt to stand on our own. I guarantee that things will be a lot easier if you ask for God's help.

If you are feeling broken right now, remember that He promises to be close to you. He will save those of you who are crushed in spirit. He does not abandon you during your time of need. You are never alone, even when you *feel* alone.

God is omnipresent and sees everything. He is omniscient (He knows all), including how best to help you. God is also omnipotent (all-powerful). He is mighty and strong beyond your imagination.

Trust and faith must carry you through your struggle. In John 12:24, the Word gives us an understanding as to *why* each person must break, or die to self. It is only in dying that we can sow seeds, which will, in the proper season, bear fruit. He will give you the grace and mercy needed to accomplish whatever He is asking of you.

By keeping your eyes on your Savior, not your circumstances, you will have the power, skills, and means to face each day. Our God warns us not to look too far into the future because it will overwhelm us. Each day carries enough worries and woes, He says.

Determine to listen to His voice daily and ask Him what He wants you to learn from your day. Meditate on the lesson your hardship is teaching you, and strive to apply it to your life. Make it your personal goal to bless others with the wisdom you have gained by walking through your trial.

Sadly, if we do not learn the lessons God has prepared for us, other circumstances will present themselves. He loves us enough not to leave us in kindergarten. He wants us to move up to first grade and all the way through college ... and even beyond!

If one storm-like setting is not successful in breaking your will or sin habit, then God will design another storm to once again present the same lesson He wants you to grasp. He loves the remedial student as much as the A+ student. He has no "teacher's pet"; we are all equal in His eyes. It is simply a matter of how quickly you want to get through "school." There are more responsibilities assigned to those who have moved past grade school, but there are also greater riches to be gained through spiritual maturity.

When you have a broken bone in your body and it is not properly set, doctors may have to rebreak the bone in order to align and heal it. If a broken leg bone is not set properly, then mobility will be hindered, leaving the wounded individual a cripple. Consider this a metaphor illuminating your spiritual growth. Refusing to submit to the will of God will expose you to more storms and broken hearts. Thankfully, God heals completely and will never choose to leave you a "spiritual cripple." Your obedience will determine your gait and spiritual health.

When you die to self and accept God's will in your life, you will discover that your brokenness has allowed you to learn and grow in the fruits of the Spirit. May goodness, kindness, gentleness, peace, love, joy, patience, faithfulness, and self-control be your reward for having bravely faced your struggle. God wants only good things for His children, and so He gives only good gifts.

Change your perspective and look upon your brokenness as a thing of beauty. For God says that when we are weak, He is strong. Wear your spiritual scars as a testimony of your devotion to Him. They will be badges of honor and things of beauty once you reach your heavenly home.

Consider now this scripture that speaks of God's ability to heal.

"He heals the brokenhearted and binds up their wounds" (Psalm 147:3 NIV).

God Will Heal Your Broken Pieces

> So do not fear, for I am with you; do not be dismayed,
> for I am your God. I will strengthen you and help
> you; I will uphold you with My righteous right hand.
> (Isaiah 41:10 NIV)

When we are broken for the glory of Christ, we share not only in His sufferings but also in His rewards as well. We gain a deeper comprehension of His incredible sacrifice for us by dying a torturous death on the cross. We appreciate all the more His devotion and unconditional love. When we suffer a trial, hopefully it will draw us even closer into His loving embrace.

We are assured that our Savior will strengthen us and help us through whatever battle we face. He promises to uphold us in His very hand! With the provision of spiritual armor, we should never have any doubt about making it through obstacles. In fact, Philippians 4:13 tells us, "We can do all things through Him who strengthens us."

So, what are the rewards gained by enduring storms? Well, for one thing, your relationship and intimacy with Christ will mature. When undergoing the maturation process, which is accompanied by trials of many kinds, we gain perseverance. The process helps to complete us here on Earth and also equips us for our heavenly work in the future.

We also gain a wisdom that can be used to comfort others who are going through trials similar to our own. We must learn to take our broken pieces and request God's assistance to reassemble them in a way that is pleasing and useful to Him. We should also pray for the wisdom to apply our new knowledge and for deeper faith.

Let's review. Trials will come; there is no getting out of them. We are promised to have the provision of God's strength to persevere and make it through our trouble. He tells us, in fact commands us, not to be dismayed when troubles come and to be unafraid. He will see us through and uphold us in His hand, but faith is required on our part.

In addition to receiving the promise that God will see us through life's circumstances, we also share in the rewards He gives when we suffer for His name. We gain wisdom, perseverance, and deeper faith in and reliance on Him. We mature instead of remaining "baby Christians" dependent only on milk. Rather, we can eat solid foods, including the Bread of Life. We grow in faith and trust every time we see the Lord faithfully bringing us through personal trials and working in the lives of those around us.

Indeed, perhaps strength is not determined by one's never being broken but, rather, by the courage one draws on so as to rise from the ashes of his or her razed life. It is by willfully choosing to use the strength God offers us to heal our broken places that we find encouragement and a deeper relationship with our Father.

Following are two Bible verses for your contemplation

"Consider it pure joy, my brothers and sisters, whenever you face trials of many kinds, because you know that the testing of your faith produces perseverance. Let perseverance finish its work so that you may be mature and complete, not lacking anything. If any of you lacks wisdom, you should ask God, who gives generously to all without finding fault, and it will be given to you" (James 1:2-5 NIV).

"For He has not despised or scorned the suffering of the afflicted one; He has not hidden His face from him but has listened to his cry for help" (Psalm 22:24 NIV).

CHAPTER 15

GOD'S PLAN AND PURPOSE

Cheryl Zelenka

The Unique Ways and Thoughts of God

> You intended to harm me, but God intended it for good to accomplish what is now being done, the saving of many lives. (Genesis 50:20 NIV)

> "For My thoughts are not your thoughts, neither are your ways My ways," declares the Lord. "As the heavens are higher than the earth, so are My ways higher than your ways and My thoughts than your thoughts." (Isaiah 55:8-9 NIV)

The ways of God can often seem illogical to humankind. But then, His ways are not our ways, and His thoughts are not our thoughts. We dare not presume to understand His plan of action in our lives. It should be enough to rest in the knowledge that He loves us and has plans to help, not harm, us.

Forget about dictating to God your ideas about how to get things done. He has a plan for your life and has orchestrated a way to accomplish it. He does not need your help planning the journey or navigating the course. He is sovereign, and He has His own way of working all things together for our good. However, what He does ask for is your obedience and trust.

God has the ability to take the evil intent of others and work it out for good and for His glory. His plans for you cannot be cast aside or dismantled. Even in the face of overwhelming circumstances, His will and His plans cannot be thwarted. His purposes will always be accomplished in His perfect timing.

Think about the story of Moses. When the astrologers told Pharaoh that Israel's redeemer (liberator) was about to be born, Pharaoh issued a decree to have all the Jewish male babies cast into the river and killed. However, God's plans and purposes are always fulfilled. Therefore, in spite of Pharaoh's death decree, Moses was rescued from his baby basket on the Nile. In living, Moses was later able to lead God's people out of slavery and bondage.

The things that happen to you in this lifetime are all a part of God's attempt to transform you into the image of His Son. Nothing that happens to you is by chance. God's purpose is never thwarted, and it often differs from the purposes of people. His ways are higher than our ways.

Sometimes, God will intervene in order to accomplish His purpose. When God initiates circumstances, it is often to encourage the believer to develop a deeper dependence on Him. Therefore it can be said that He wants to care for you. He wants to put you in situations where you can witness His doing mighty works. He desires your praise and will provide many opportunities in your life for you to acknowledge His power and strength.

Take some time to reflect upon the following scripture and quote by A.W. Tozer

> "The Lord of hosts has sworn, saying, "Surely, as I have thought, so it shall come to pass, and as I have purposed, so it shall stand." Isaiah 14:24 (NKJV)

> "By regeneration and sanctification, by faith and prayer, by suffering and discipline, by the Word and the Spirit, the work goes on till the dream of God has been realized in the Christian heart."[1]—A.W. Tozer

Don't Light the Fire When God Has the Matches!

> But now, all you who light fires and provide yourselves with flaming torches, go, walk in the light of your fires and of the torches you have set ablaze. This is what you shall receive from my hand: You will lie down in torment. (Isaiah 50:11 NIV)

Do you like being in control of all situations? Are you frustrated when you can't be the leader? Is this because you have been let down and disappointed by others? Do you feel that you are the only one capable of getting things done properly, that you are the only person you can rely on and trust?

We have all been disappointed by people. Humans are flawed. We often have good intentions, but life events can get in the way, and we either forget things or sweep them aside. Intentionally or unintentionally, we disappoint friends and loved ones, and they disappoint us. This is where we have to hope that God's forgiveness will override our selfish or forgetful actions. Often we do not even realize the depth to which we have wounded others or to which others have disappointed us.

When you are the one who is overlooked, your disappointment regarding others' unreliable behavior can harden your heart. With damaged trust, you might become self-reliant and decide not to wait on the Lord for direction. Like a bounding puppy, you may even run ahead of the Lord, doing whatever feels good or going wherever your feet may lead. But you are deceiving yourself if you think that you don't need others or God in your life.

We are the body of Christ. This means that we are precious individual parts that make up a whole. God is the Head. He created us to be dependent on each other. In order to function properly, each individual needs to share his or her gifts, using them to bless and help the other parts of the body of Christ. God created us to interact and have a relationship not only with Him, but also with each other. It is a lie from the Enemy that you are better off alone and can take care of yourself.

Our Enemy is a prowling lion just waiting to find a lamb that has wandered off alone to graze in some isolated pasture. When the flock sticks together, it is harder for the Enemy to attack. Don't let the failures of others, and the resultant disappointment it causes, separate you from the fold.

Not sharing yourself with others is selfish. Reasons for it are fear and insecurity. When you stand alone as an island, you are choosing to withhold your love, talents, and blessings. It is faulty thinking that leads you to step out of your dependence on God and others. You may think you don't need "them," but you do—and they most certainly need you. God teaches us through relationships. Any time fear is the motivating influence behind your actions, step back and rethink things. Perfect love casts out all fear (1 John 4:18)!

Finally, don't let the temptation to be self-reliant affect your relationship with God. He is in control. He will never disappoint you, even though you will need faith to accept His will in some matters of your life. Believing He has good things in store for you and knowing that His ways may require you to travel in a direction other than the one you desire will help you to accept His leading. Don't be foolish and run ahead of God. He is the leader, the Good Shepherd. He will gather and lead His flock on a safe path. Eventually, He will lead you to green pastures so that you may feed. He will provide for you, in His time and in His way. Let Him take care of your needs and provide for you. He is dependable and trustworthy. Hope in Him, and remember that hope will never disappoint (Romans 5:5).

These three Bible verses will help you in your meditation:

"Those who trust in themselves are fools, but those who walk in wisdom are kept safe" (Proverbs 28:26 NIV).

"My sheep listen to my voice; I know them, and they follow me" (John 10:27 NIV).

"There is no fear in love. But perfect love drives out fear, because fear has to do with punishment. The one who fears is not made perfect in love" (John 4:18 NIV).

CHAPTER 16

CONTROL

All-Free Downloads by Dave

Who Is Leading the Procession?

> But thanks be to God, who always leads us as captives in Christ's triumphal procession and uses us to spread the aroma of the knowledge of Him everywhere. (2 Corinthians 2:14 NIV)

> This is what the Lord says—your Redeemer, the Holy One of Israel: "I am the Lord your God, who teaches you what is best for you, who directs you in the way you should go." (Isaiah 48:17 NIV)

Why do we always want to get in front of God and lead? Why do we insist on running ahead and telling Him which direction to turn or where to stop the parade? Why do we, the creation, insist on telling our Creator what to do? How did we become so prideful and arrogant? Do we really think that we are better off driving the car or leading the way? After all, God has the map, compass, and plan of action.

When it comes to our personal lives, most of us have goals we want to achieve. We have mapped out our futures and developed a plan of action. Too often, we forget to include God in our schemes. Attempting to accomplish personal goals and well-thought-out plans, without adding God into the equation, will surely end in frustration. He has a purpose and plan for us, and we need to be attentive to His leading, even when it does not align with our vision.

Letting God direct your steps means that you lay down your will and relinquish all attempts to control your own life. Trusting God will enable you to fall back and allow Him to guide you in the exciting procession called life. He will show you which way to go and teach you what is best for you.

As you hand over the reins of your life and trust in His skills as a navigator, your desires will align themselves to His perfect will. It is only then that He will grant you all the desires of your heart. Because you have delighted yourself in Him and found peace in His will for you, He will act. He will act on your behalf by providing blessings and lessons that mature you in your faith.

When we surrender our personal plans for the future and ask the Father to make His will our will, we experience transformation. A sort of "revival" will rumble within us, and an inexplicable peace will become our cloak. When we accept that our future no longer belongs to us, and when we lay it down before God as an offering of gratitude, a sweet aroma will arise before Him. This aroma, much like incense before His throne, is an indication that He accepts your offering as a pleasing sacrifice.

There are some who call the laying down of one's will "a little death." In reality, it is a glorious resurrection of spirit. It is an acceptance of all to come. Contentment will fill you as you submit. Peace will come, too, as you fully comprehend that wherever He leads you, even into the valley of the shadow of death, you need not fear any evil there. In the procession called your life, He will faithfully guide you through and, eventually, all the way to your eternal home.

These two Bible quotes are for your meditation:

"Many are the plans in a person's heart, but it is the Lord's purpose that prevails" (Proverbs 19:21 NIV).

"Delight yourself in the Lord, and He will give you the desires of your heart. Commit your way to the Lord; trust in Him, and He will act" (Psalm 37:4-5 NIV).

Cheryl Zelenka

Don't Run Ahead of God

> And our wise Father in heaven knows when we're going to need things, too. *Don't run out ahead of him* [emphasis added].[1]—Corrie ten Boom

> My sheep listen to my voice; I know them, and they follow Me. (John 10:27 NIV)

Are you one who likes to lead and be in control of everything in your life? Is this because you have been let down and disappointed by others, and now you feel that you are the only one capable of getting things done properly? You won't let yourself down, so you—and you alone—can be trusted, right? *Wrong!*

People have disappointed us *all*. Humans are flawed. We often have good intentions, but life can get in the way, leading us to forget things and sweep them aside. Intentionally or unintentionally, we disappoint friends and loved ones. This is where we have to hope that people's forgiveness will override our selfish actions. We may not even realize how much we have disappointed the person we neglected.

When we are overlooked, our lack of faith in the reliability of others will harden us. Our trust is damaged, so we become self-reliant and forget to wait on the Lord for direction. Like bounding puppies, we run ahead of the Lord, go where we please, and do what feels good. We think we don't need others to fend for us. We can take care of ourselves so the hurt of being let down won't wound us ever again.

But God created us as a body. He wants us to help and fellowship with each other. He does not want us to isolate ourselves. The

Enemy is a prowling lion just waiting to find a lamb that has wondered off and is grazing alone in a pasture. When the flock sticks together, it is harder for the Enemy to attack. Don't let the failure of others and the disappointment it causes you separate you from the fold.

In addition, don't let the desire for self-reliance affect your relationship with God. He is in control. He will never disappoint you, even though you need to have faith and accept His will in some matters. Believing He has good things planned for you and knowing that His ways may require you to go in a direction other than the one you would choose will help you to accept His leading. Don't be foolish and run ahead of God. He is the leader, the Good Shepherd. He will gather His flock, show them the safe path to follow, and lead them to a green pasture to feed. He will provide, in His time and in His way.

"Your word is a lamp for my feet, a light on my path" (Psalm 119:105 NIV).

CHAPTER 17

WORRY AND ANXIETY

> Matthew 6:34
> Therefore do not worry about tomorrow, for tomorrow will worry about itself. Each day has enough trouble of its own.

By Hear Jesus Christ

That Nasty Villain Named Worry

> Do not fret—it leads only to evil. (Psalm 37:8b NIV)

> Do not be anxious about anything, but in everything, by prayer and petition, with thanksgiving, present your requests to God. And the peace of God, which transcends all understanding, will guard your hearts and your minds in Christ Jesus. (Philippians 4:6-7 NIV)

That nasty villain named worry will often sneak into our dreams and rob us of sleep. How many of you know him and suffer from his harassments? You can battle this enemy in several ways and regain your peace.

Memorizing Scripture that addresses anxiety and fear is a powerful tool. It takes time and requires some review, but it is worth the investment. The Holy Spirit will faithfully recall these memorized verses when you are in need. He will also bring them to mind when you have an opportunity to encourage another with His words.

Since Satan is unable to read your mind, it is wise to recite the passages out loud when anxiety strikes. Hearing the words will comfort and calm you. It will also give the Enemy an earful. The Word tells us in James 4:7 that if we resist the Devil, he will flee. This is a promise!

God, as our teacher, is always pleased by His children's efforts to apply new knowledge. It is never too late to learn something new and to put into practice.

Philippians 4:6-7 is an especially powerful verse to memorize. It reminds us to "be anxious about nothing." It continues by instructing believers to approach God in prayer with a thankful heart regarding their worries. This thankfulness comes from knowing that God hears every prayer and is in control. And what is the promised result of following these instructions? A peace that transcends all understanding!

When worry and anxiety start to strangle you, fear is often not far behind. Trusting in God's love and faithfulness will help you by renewing your strength. Reflecting on the might of God, the Creator of the universe, will remind you that He has incredible power. He sees all, knows all, and will handle all in His perfect timing and ways.

Memorizing Scripture and meditating on His power can eliminate anxiety and worry. However, there are other ways to battle your anxious thoughts. Why not reflect on all of the ways God has shown Himself as a faithful Father? Reflect on all the problems in your past and how they have been resolved. If God helped you to solve problems back then, then He will certainly do so in the present and in your future.

God is always in command. Who better to take care of your troubles? Don your spiritual armor, including the sword, which is the Word of God. It helps in your battles with the Evil One. Don't forget that you are fighting a spiritual battle every day. Satan, that prowling lion, looks for every opportunity to confuse and harass you. He wants to steal your peace. Don't give him any ground! Put on your armor, resist him, praise and thank God, recite all the ways He has shown Himself faithful and true, pray, and keep your spiritual sword sharp! Worry does not have to paralyze you.

Facing Trials: Thoughts For Meditation

Trust God and be not afraid. Give all your worries and cares to God. He cares so much for you.

Here are three passages for your meditation:

"Cast all your anxiety on Him because He cares for you" (1 Peter 5:7 NIV).

"Therefore do not worry about tomorrow, for tomorrow will worry about itself. Each day has enough trouble of its own" (Matthew 6:34 NIV).

"Submit yourselves, then, to God. Resist the devil, and he will flee from you" (James 4:7 NIV).

The Anxiety of Mary

> Mary lived in invisibility in the moments of an ordinary, obscure life, as far as anyone in her own life knew. And yet, in the living of her life, quietly, faithfully, God noticed her ... God saw her and she found favor and pleased His heart. God always sees ... Even when no one else is noticing.[1]—Sally Clarkson

> But make up your mind not to worry beforehand how you will defend yourselves. For I will give you words and wisdom that none of your adversaries will be able to resist or contradict. (Luke 21:14 NIV)

Do you ever feel invisible? Do you ever feel like you are so ordinary that nobody, not even God, would notice you or use you for a purpose? If so, be encouraged by the story of Mary, the woman chosen to give birth to the Savior of the world.

The Virgin Mary lived her life in quiet faithfulness. God noticed her as she lived her day-to-day life. The Bible does not remark that she was a great beauty, like Esther was. Nor was Mary an incredibly intelligent and gifted young woman, at least not as far as we know. She did not have to be talented or outwardly beautiful to get God's attention. Her simple faith and goodness is what earned her the favor of our Creator.

The favor came at a great cost to this young woman, though. The trials she underwent would put many of our more petty sufferings to shame. We ought to find encouragement in Mary's perseverance and faith to accept the path God decided to lead her on. She did not shout from the rooftops that she was carrying the

Savior of the world in her womb. No, it was with quiet submission that she accepted the will of God.

Mary must have felt great anxiety when facing her betrothed with the news of her pregnancy. Joseph had not known her intimately, and he had decided to divorce her quietly. God provided for Mary by sending an angel to Joseph in a dream. In Matthew 1:20, the angel said, "Joseph son of David, do not be afraid to take Mary home as your wife, because what is conceived in her is from the Holy Spirit. She will give birth to a Son, and you are to give Him the name Jesus, because He will save His people from their sins."

When Joseph woke from his dream, he did what the angel had commanded and took Mary home as his wife. Any worry Mary had felt was set aside by God's provision and grace. Protection had been provided.

Throughout Mary's life, God was there to provide for her. The birth of her son occurred within walls, not in the great outdoors. A lowly manger was the Savior's bed, but it was God's provision and sufficient for Mary's needs.

Shortly after the wise men had left their gifts with the newborn Savior, a new crisis erupted for Mary and Joseph. Herod had heard about the birth of a new ruler for Israel. He sent out an order to kill all the boys in Bethlehem who were two years old and younger.

Matthew 2:13 continues the story: "When they [the magi] had gone, an angel of the Lord appeared to Joseph in a dream. 'Get up,' he said, 'take the child and his mother and escape to Egypt. Stay there until I tell you, for Herod is going to search for the child to kill him.' So he got up, took the child and his mother during the night and left for Egypt, where he stayed until the death of Herod."

Mary had to set aside her worry and instead trust that God would protect the Son He had given her through the Holy Spirit. Since the message to leave Bethlehem had come to Joseph, Mary also had to trust that God was leading her through her husband.

Mary found favor in God's eyes through her quiet faithfulness. She did not go unnoticed. Her obedience, her submitting to God's eternal plan, could have led her to suffer many nights in anxiety. Instead, Mary exercised her trust in His goodness and provision. She threw her cares back up to her heavenly Father and depended on Him to protect her and lead her throughout life.

If God is for you, who can be against you (Romans 8:31)? If you submit to His will for your life, He will be faithful to complete the work that He has begun in you. Mary's purpose was to give birth to and raise the Son of Man. She did not let worry interfere with that purpose. She did not let the fear of humankind or circumstances rob her of the honor God had offered.

Remember Mary and all she had to face the next time worry visits your doorstep. Consider her act of faith and submit to the trial before you, knowing that God will take care of any problem that challenges you. He is looking for the faithful to cast their cares upon Him. His shoulders are just about as wide as his arm span; they are as far as the east is from the west.

Facing Trials: Thoughts For Meditation

These two Bible passages are provided for your meditation:

"I sought the Lord, and He answered me; He delivered me from all my fears" (Psalm 34:4 NIV).

"The angel went to her and said, 'Greetings, you who are highly favored! The Lord is with you'" (Luke 1:28 NIV).

(The description of *highly favored* comes from a single Greek word, which essentially means *much grace*.)

CHAPTER 18

HOPE

> *My soul,*
> *wait in silence for God only,*
> *For my hope is from Him.*
> *Psalm 62:5*

By Trust Him Always

There Is Always Hope

> God is the only one who can make the valley of trouble a door of hope.[1]—Catherine Marshall

> May the God of hope fill you with all joy and peace as you trust in Him, so that you may overflow with hope by the power of the Holy Spirit. (Romans 15:13 NIV)

Where is your *door of hope* these days? Has trouble and suffering knocked you off your feet and left you in the dark? There is no need for you to worry, as hope is birthed in the dark.

Hardships can blind even the strongest of Christians, leaving them hopeless and in the dark. Maturity in Christ comes through trials. James 1:1-4 tells us, "Count it pure joy when we encounter trials of many kids, for the testing of our faith develops perseverance." Hope and perseverance go hand in hand. They are sisters. We need hope in order to persevere through a trial.

Satan loves to rob a Christian of his or her hope. The Devil has many means to do this, but depression is a tool he often likes to utilize. Depression is a black pit. It is a painful and dark place where hope has trouble communicating with us. If we struggle with a chemical or genetic imbalance, then recovery is all the more difficult. Yes, difficult—but not impossible! God is the Great Physician and our *healer*.

Depression is as painful as a tumor or cancer. Even the most devout Christians can fall prey to this painful condition. The depressed will often suffer from personal guilt and fall victim to the projected condemnation of fellow believers.

God understands the grief that comes from loss or hardships. Jesus is called the Man of Sorrows, as He is acquainted with grief. We need to gird ourselves with the full protection of the armor of Christ when we are in the valley of the shadow of death. This task may be exhausting for a depressed individual, but it will really pay off. Fiery darts flung by the Enemy will bounce off the spiritual armor and keep a person from falling even deeper into Satan's pit of hopelessness.

God understands your sorrow and grief. He does not condemn you for your emotions. He gave you the emotions and will teach you how to master them, if you let Him. He wants to help pull you out of your dark pit.

Now there is a warning to all believers: "judge not, lest you yourself be judged." Remember, when you point a finger of judgment at someone, there are three fingers pointing right back at you. Be sure to take the plank out of your own eye before mentioning the splinter in another's eye. Compassion will carry us all farther into healing than a judgmental spirit will. In other words, it is un-Christian to negatively judge a person who suffers from clinical depression.

Still, the depressed individual must take hold of responsibility and work toward his or her own healing. Though depression robs a person of energy, we have all been given the same effective tools for battle. If you suffer from depression, then pray to God and ask for His help. Sing worship songs or play them on your radio. Read your Bible; listen to a podcast or a radio sermon. God will speak to you even when you can't read the Word yourself. Trust in God's ability to touch you with His healing hands. Rejoice in knowing that there is always hope for a child of the living God.

Facing Trials: Thoughts For Meditation

These two Bible quotes will aid you in your meditations:

"Rejoice in hope, be patient in tribulation, be constant in prayer" (Romans 12:12 NIV).

"Though He slay me, yet will I hope in Him; I will surely defend my ways to His face" (Job 13:15 NIV).

Cheryl Zelenka

Hope Will Move You Forward

> If you'll quit moaning and crying, I'll use the things [trials] to make you into someone I can use in the lives of others; to show them that no matter where they've been, no matter how deep the hole, no matter how painful the trial, there's hope. There is victory.[2]—Kay Arthur

> For in this hope we were saved. But hope that is seen is no hope at all. Who hopes for what they already have? But if we hope for what we do not yet have, we wait for it patiently. (Romans 8:24-25)

Hope provides us with the strength to take one more step forward. Hope will motivate the weariest of believers to continue along the path on which God has placed them. It will never disappoint. It is tied to faith and love. If we love God, then we have faith in what is hoped for—and we are certain of what is unseen.

After the flood, God gave Noah a promise and a hope. We can still see the outcome of His promise today, in the lovely shape of a rainbow after a storm.

Storms are difficult and rocky. They will toss a believer back and forth and test his or her endurance. They are meant to build spiritual muscles and our dependence on God. He wants us to rely on Him and not on our own abilities, which He gave us in the first place.

Hope is a feeling of expectation and a desire for a certain thing to happen. Hope requires trust and a belief that promises will be kept.

Facing Trials: Thoughts For Meditation

It is with anticipation that hopes are realized.

If you are working your way through a trial right now and you feel hopeless about your situation, consider this fact. Satan is a thief and wants to rob you of hope. If hope is lost, then so is motivation and desire. Hopelessness leaves us weak and powerless against the schemes of the Enemy. Hopelessness gives him the upper hand. In addition, hopelessness disregards the power of God.

The Creator of the universe can do all things. He is all-powerful. We can do all things through Him, who gives us strength (Philippians 4:13). Because of this promise alone, we should never lose hope. Even when things appear dark and impossible to solve, we must remember that God is the God who makes the impossible possible.

Kay Arthur reminds us, in the quote above, to stop our complaining about difficult circumstances and trials, as God will use them to mold us. God's willing servant will use the lessons learned from a trial to encourage others. This servant in now equipped to provide tangible hope for others, thanks to the faithfulness, comfort, and hope God has shown him or her from the very start.

We can rest in our hope that God's grace is sufficient to carry us through fires and rough waters. Our endurance will increase through our difficult trials, honing our character into one full of hope.

These three Scripture quotes will serve to edify you through meditation:

"Through whom we have gained access by faith into this grace in which we now stand. And we boast in the hope of the glory of God. Not only so, but we also glory in our sufferings, because we know that suffering produces perseverance; perseverance, character; and character, hope. And hope does not put us to shame, because God's love has been poured out into our hearts through the Holy Spirit, who has been given to us" (Romans 5:2-5 NIV).

"I can do all things through Him who gives me strength" (Philippians 4:13 NIV).

"Be joyful in hope, patient in affliction, faithful in prayer" (Romans 12:12 NIV).

CHAPTER 19

WISDOM

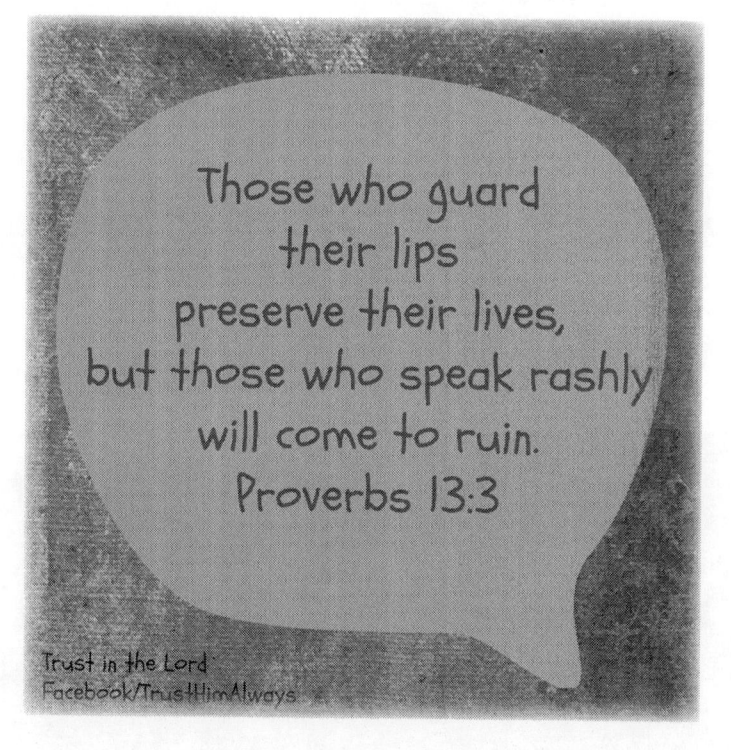

> Those who guard
> their lips
> preserve their lives,
> but those who speak rashly
> will come to ruin.
> Proverbs 13:3
>
> Trust in the Lord
> Facebook/TrustHimAlways

By Trust Him Always

A Wise Person Knows When to Speak

> A *smart* person knows what to say. A *wise* person knows whether or not to say it. —Unknown

> The wise in heart are called discerning, and pleasant words promote instruction. (Proverbs 16:21 NIV)

> Reckless words pierce like a sword, but the tongue of the wise brings healing. (Proverbs 12:18 NIV)

The book of Proverbs is full of wisdom. The gems inside it are there for you to grab and implant into your heart.

One of the many nuggets of gold found in the Word of God is in Proverbs 12:18, which speaks of the human being's tongue and the power it holds. The tongue is something that can offer up healing or serve up pain and suffering. It is the fool who speaks before listening. In fact, Proverbs 29:20 tells us that a person who speaks in haste has less hope than a fool. Furthermore, Proverbs 21:23 adds that if you guard your mouth and tongue, you will avoid calamity.

When somebody is suffering a loss and feeling grief of some sort, friends and family want to offer comfort through words and actions. Unfortunately, well-meant words can often cause more harm than good. In times of tragedy, it is sometimes better to remain silent. A kind glance or a compassionate embrace can be more comforting than a well-intentioned but misspoken word. Remaining silent requires self-control. Actions of service and love will surely be a comfort to your friend in need.

Facing Trials: Thoughts For Meditation

There are times when you see a believer in sin and you want to rebuke him or her. You recall that Proverbs 27:6 says, "The wounds of a friend can be trusted, but an enemy multiplies kisses." Do these words give you the freedom to speak a rebuke every time you see sin? *No!* However, they do give you permission to *pray*. You might not be the person appointed by God to address another's sin. There may be another person appointed by God who needs to share a loving word of concern. It could be that this is a special person who will have a positive influence on the sinner. If you speak without the leading of the Holy Spirit, then you may turn a sinner into a deeper state of rebellion or despair.

Finally, Matthew 12:36 reminds us that on the Day of Judgment, we will have to give an account of every one of our carelessly spoken words. This verse alone is enough to make any person seriously consider taking a vow of silence for the rest of his or her life! There have been many senseless, useless, and careless words spoken by many a tongue. Sadly, we can't take them back, but we can certainly confess them to God and strive to be more careful with our words.

Try to recall a time when you were full of sorrow and a well-intentioned but misspoken word was sent your way, causing you even deeper pain and agony. What could the person have done instead to help you along in your healing? Is this a possible life lesson for you? Could it be that you have also unintentionally wounded a person in pain with reckless words, speaking before considering the impact?

Overall, people are too quick to speak their minds, judge actions, and give advice. Try to listen more and speak less. Let your words be few, and as a result you will find that when you *do* speak, many will listen with their undivided attention.

Cheryl Zelenka

Following are three Bible verses for your reflection:

"He who guards his mouth and his tongue keeps himself from calamity" (Proverbs 21:23 NIV).

"Do you see someone who speaks in haste? There is more hope for a fool than for them" (Proverbs 29:20 NIV).

"I tell you, on the Day of Judgment people will give account for every careless word they speak" (Matthew 12:36 ESV).

How to Obtain Wisdom

> The beginning of wisdom is this: Get wisdom. Though it cost all you have, get understanding. (Proverbs 4:7 NIV)

> My goal is that they may be encouraged in heart and united in love, so that they may have the full riches of complete understanding, in order that they may know the mystery of God, namely, Christ, in whom are hidden all the treasures of wisdom and knowledge. (Colossians 2:2-3 NIV)

> The fear of the Lord is the beginning of wisdom; all who follow His precepts have good understanding. To Him belongs eternal praise. (Psalm 111:10 NIV)

The fear of the Lord is a reverent respect for God. It is the starting point for anyone seeking to gain wisdom. The entire fourth proverb is about the importance of gaining wisdom. Wisdom is supreme and worth far more than rubies and gold. It is a fool who does not seek the treasures found within wisdom's bounty. So how does one acquire wisdom, and what exactly are its benefits? Job 12:12 offers a hint. The verse begins, "Wisdom is with the aged."

It is through life experiences that we gain wisdom. Trials we suffer and difficult struggles we undergo add to our measure of wisdom. The older we are, the more storms we have weathered. We can learn so much from the elders among us who have passed through difficult times similar to our own. Proverb 4:1 starts out commanding sons to listen attentively to their father's instruction, for through it they will gain understanding.

Wisdom brings with her more benefits than can be listed on this page. However, one of her merits includes the ability to preserve life. Wisdom enables us to apply knowledge, allowing us to find a way out of tight spots. She also guides and protects us. Wisdom is to be loved and cherished, especially since she will faithfully watch over those in her care.

James 3:17 attributes gentle traits to ~~Wisdom~~ wisdom by referring to her as: peaceful, sincere, impartial, and full of mercy. With ~~Wisdom~~ wisdom there will come good fruits. You will recognize her wisdom in those who listen to advice and apply it with an even hand.

Where are all the hidden treasures of wisdom and knowledge to be found? They are buried as treasure in Christ Jesus. As you build your relationship with Christ, He will unveil more and more of His mysteries and wisdom. The wisdom that comes from heaven is pure, and it is those who are pure of heart that hunger for it.

Call out for ~~Wisdom~~ wisdom, without doubting the One who escorts her ~~it~~ your way. Expect her arrival with anticipation and with longing. Once ~~she Wisdom~~ has arrived, be carefully in how you greet her ~~it~~, since you do not want to lose her favor. As a gentleman walks with his lady, so must you with ~~Wisdom~~ Wisdom. Make the best use of your time with ~~her~~ wisdom, for ~~its~~ her company is highly sought after and greatly valued. Give Wisdom your undivided attention, and you will be richly rewarded with blessings and a long, merciful life.

Meditate on the verse below and consider the value of gaining wisdom.

"Blessed are those who find wisdom, those who gain understanding, for she is more profitable than silver and yields better returns than gold. She is more precious than rubies; nothing you desire can compare with her. Long life is in her right hand; in her left hand are riches and honor. Her ways are pleasant ways, and all her paths are peace. She is a tree of life to those who take hold of her; those who hold her fast will be blessed" (Proverbs 3:13-18 NIV).

CHAPTER 20

WALKING WITH THE SPIRIT OF GOD

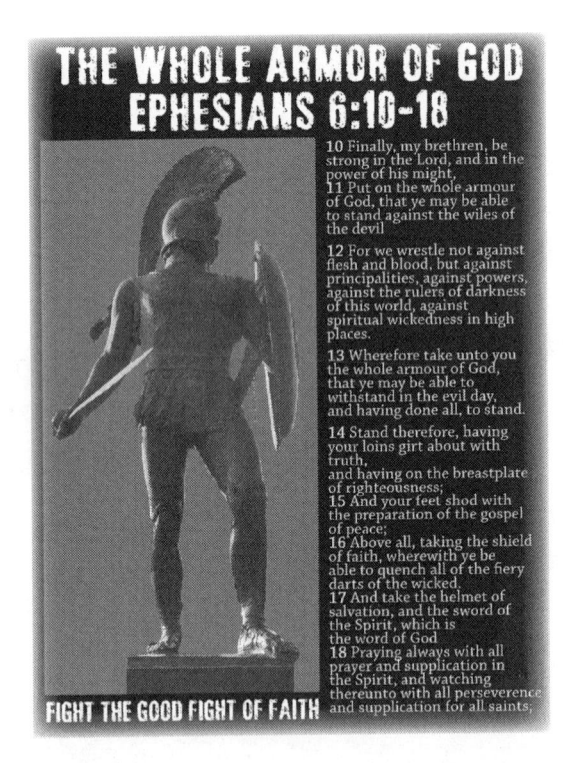

THE WHOLE ARMOR OF GOD
EPHESIANS 6:10-18

10 Finally, my brethren, be strong in the Lord, and in the power of his might.
11 Put on the whole armour of God, that ye may be able to stand against the wiles of the devil.

12 For we wrestle not against flesh and blood, but against principalities, against powers, against the rulers of darkness of this world, against spiritual wickedness in high places.

13 Wherefore take unto you the whole armour of God, that ye may be able to withstand in the evil day, and having done all, to stand.

14 Stand therefore, having your loins girt about with truth, and having on the breastplate of righteousness;
15 And your feet shod with the preparation of the gospel of peace;
16 Above all, taking the shield of faith, wherewith ye be able to quench all of the fiery darts of the wicked.
17 And take the helmet of salvation, and the sword of the Spirit, which is the word of God
18 Praying always with all prayer and supplication in the Spirit, and watching thereunto with all perseverance and supplication for all saints;

FIGHT THE GOOD FIGHT OF FAITH

All-Free Downloads by Tony Melena

Spiritual Maturity

> One of the marks of spiritual maturity is the quiet confidence that God is in control—without the need to understand why He does what He does.—Anonymous

> And so, from the day we heard, we have not ceased to pray for you, asking that you may be filled with the knowledge of his will in all spiritual wisdom and understanding, so as to walk in a manner worthy of the Lord, fully pleasing to him, bearing fruit in every good work and increasing in the knowledge of God. (Colossians 1:9-10 ESV)

Wonderful analogies can be made regarding our need for physical and emotional growth and our need for spiritual growth. God does not want us to remain immature or in a stagnant state of ungrowth. Our physical bodies were designed to "stretch" and mature into taller, stronger, and fruitful bodies.

We are called the children of God, but this does not mean He wants us to go through life as two-year-olds. As middle-aged adults, we will always remain children in the eyes of our parents. However, there is nothing attractive or appealing in adults who refuse to grow up emotionally. Responsibilities can be scary and intimidating. However, it is necessary that we take them on if we want to become who God intended us to be. To remain a child emotionally, even though our bodies have matured, is a disappointment to God.

Spiritual maturity is a commendable goal. When the Holy Spirit fills you with the knowledge of His will, you are able to walk in a manner worthy of the Lord. This will be fully pleasing to Him, as you will bear fruit in every good work you do for His glory.

God wants you to deepen your relationship with Him by increasing your knowledge of Him. Our maturity in Christ will come at different times and speeds, however. The quickness of growth and the depth of maturity depends on a believer's willingness to submit to God and lay aside his or her will in favor of God's plans. Making the choice to trust God's direction and purpose for us will often happen when we experience deep brokenness and maintain a faith strengthened by storms. Trials teach us to exercise our spiritual muscles so that we develop perseverance.

There are many markers used to identify the mature Christian. An unswervable faith that does not require explanations from God is a good indicator. It is so tempting to throw up whys to our heavenly Father. In the long run, though, *why* does not matter if our faith is rooted in the fact that we serve a loving God who has plans to prosper us and provide us with a hopeful future. Mature believers live by the promise of Romans 2:28: "And we know that in all things God works for the good of those who love Him, who have been called according to His purpose."

Mature Christians live their lives looking for opportunities to serve others and God. Selfishness may rear its ugly head on occasion, but a mature Christian finds joy in putting others first. The fruits of the Spirit thereby manifests themselvesitself. And although sin will always plague believers, it will not rule the heart of a mature believer. Therefore, goodness, kindness, gentleness, peace, love, joy, patience, faithfulness, and self-control will allow those who are mature in Christ to be living testimonies to the world.

If you are tired of being tossed around by doubt and indecision or fear and anger, then lay down your personal agenda. Stop asking God why and start praying, "Use me!"

"Then we will no longer be infants, tossed back and forth by the waves, and blown here and there by every wind of teaching and by the cunning and craftiness of people in their deceitful scheming. Instead, speaking the truth in love, we will grow to become in every respect the mature body of Him who is the Head, that is, Christ" (Ephesians 4:14-15 NIV).

Confusion Is *Not* of the Lord

> For God is not the author of confusion, but of peace (1 Corinthians 14:33 NIV).

> "For My thoughts are not your thoughts, neither are your ways My ways," declares the Lord. "As the heavens are higher than the earth, so are My ways higher than your ways and My thoughts than your thoughts." (Isaiah 55:8-9 NIV)

There are times in a Christian's walk when confusion attacks and leaves the believer frozen in his or her tracks. The questions in his or her mind seem to turn into a demonic cloud of smoke, blinding all vision and understanding. Thus, progress in the person's journey comes to a complete standstill.

The Word of God instructs us to be wise to the Enemy and his schemes. Matthew 10:16 warns us that we are living among wolves and are to be as shrewd as snakes while maintaining our innocence. We cannot stick our heads in the sand and pretend evil is not all around us.

If you are experiencing confusion in your prayer life, it is probably because of one of several reasons. It could be that Satan is harassing and attacking you. This will often occur when a saint makes some kind of progress in regaining ground which the Evil One had formerly won. Confusion is never of the Lord, so get in the habit of dressing yourself in the armor of Christ and sharpening your sword, which is, of course, the living Word.

The Bible promises us that if we submit to God and resist the Devil, the Devil must flee from our very presence. We are in a battle down here on Earth, and as such we cannot be complacent while we journey. *Resist* is defined as "to withstand, strive against, or oppose."[1] To oppose and strive against confusion, you must pray to God and read His Word.

We are soldiers in the army of Christ. We need to exercise our spiritual muscles and increase our strength by leaning more and more on our Savior's provisions and grace. The Holy Spirit is quiet in nature but is faithful to pinch us if we are in danger or in need of instruction. Trust your discernment and practice it.

Another reason why your prayer life might have you confused is because you have unknowingly put God in a box. "His thoughts are not our thoughts, neither are our ways His ways" (Isaiah 55:8-9). His ways are so much better than our ways! Could your seemingly unanswered prayers already have been answered? He loves doing the unexpected, and so He could have answered (or will soon answer) your petition in a way you never had imagined. Look deeper into your supplications and examine if there has been an unexpected change in your life. Is it possible that the change is an answer to your prayer?

Finally, consider if timing plays a part in the answering of your prayers. God keeps time in a different manner than we do here on Earth. He has appointed times for all people and events. Psalm 31:5 informs us that our times are in His hands. Since humans are impatient, our waiting for anything seems unbearable. However, there are many reasons why God may not respond to a prayer immediately. He may have our safety in mind when he waits before delivering as promised. Consider the possibility that terrible accidents or life-threatening moments have been avoided because God intervened. Maybe we had to wait an extra minute at a red light when driving and missed a huge traffic wreck as a result. Maybe we had to work a bit of overtime and thus avoided calamity.

God is our *master teacher,* and we are His *students.* When He sees our heads tilted to the side and notices the "huh?" in our glance, He will be faithful to reteach His lessons. Today His lesson was about identifying confusion in your prayer life and removing it. Prayer and the use of Scripture is always the best way to overcome the schemes and lies of the Enemy. Take heart, and never hesitate to cry out to God when confusion strikes.

Following are three quotes for you to reflect on during your meditation:

"Submit yourselves, then, to God. Resist the devil, and he will flee from you" (James 4:7 NIV).

"I am sending you out like sheep among wolves. Therefore be as shrewd as snakes and as innocent as doves" (Matthew 10:16 NIV).

"No one is a firmer believer in the power of prayer than the devil; not that he practices it, but he suffers from it."[2]—Guy H. King

About the Author

Cheryl Zelenka taught in the public school system for over twenty-five years. She is the single parent of one adopted son, a former fourth grade student. In July of 2011, her parents realized her health was quickly deteriorating and insisted that she visit their doctor in Arizona. The physician immediately identified a neurological issue, which then led to the diagnosis of a noncancerous brain tumor. Upon the removal of this growth, there was an immediate change in her personality. Cheryl's recovery has been nothing less than miraculous.

Although the past two years have been full of changes and loss, Cheryl chooses to look at things with a positive attitude. "I refuse to wallow in the mud. I left behind a wonderful life in Oregon: good friends, a dream house, a great job, and a comfortable and stable life. However, I believe God has 'pruned' me and is now asking that I pen His words to encourage and instruct others. If I can take the ashes of my life and rebuild them into a thing of beauty, then you can, too."

Cheryl's second book is a Bible study called *Divine Interruptions: Opportunities for Spiritual Growth*. She shares her personal journey through the discovery of her brain tumor and aligns it with the biblical story of Job. Look for it in December 2013 on *Amazon.com*.

Read more articles by Cheryl Zelenka on the following sites:

http://facingtrials.com/
http://weepingintodancing.com/
http://vineoflife.net/ (Go to "Church/Family" and scroll to "Devotions.")
http://inspirationalchristiansfortoday.com/

NOTES

Scripture quotations designated (*AB*) are taken from *The Amplified Bible,* Old Testament. Copyright © 1965, 1987 by the Zondervan Corporation. Used by permission. All rights reserved.

Scripture quotations designated (*ESV*) are taken from *The Holy Bible, English Standard Version.* Copyright © 2000, 2001 by Crossway Bibles, a division of Good News Publishers. Used by permission. All rights reserved.

Scripture quotations designated (*NASB*) are taken from the *New American Standard Bible.* Copyright © 1960, 1962, 1963, 1968, 1971, 1972, 1973, 1975, 1977 by The Lockman Foundation. Used by permission.

Scripture quotations designated (*NIV*) are taken from the *Holy Bible: New International Version®. NIV®.* Copyright © 1973, 1978, 1984 by International Bible Society. Used by permission of Zondervan. All rights reserved.

Scripture quotations marked (*NLT*) are taken from the *Holy Bible: New Living Translation,* copyright © 1996. Used by permission of Tyndale House Publishers, Inc., Wheaton, IL 60189 USA. All rights reserved.

Chapter 1: Facing Trials

[1] *Once-a-Day Walk with Jesus Devotional: 365 Days in the New Testament.* Grand Rapids: Zondervan, 2011.
[2] "The Best Inspirational Quotes." *The Board of Wisdom.* http://boardofwisdom.com/togo/?start=3091&viewid=1005&listname=inspiration al&m=0. Accessed July 7, 2013.

Chapter 2: Broken

[1] Southerland, Mary. "The Power of One Broken Seed." Posted October 25, 2011. *The Stress-Buster and Women's Ministries Motivator.* http://www.marysoutherland.com/. Accessed July 7, 2013.

Chapter 4: Obedience

[1] Stewart, Ed, ed. *Jesus 365: A Devotional.* Eugene: Harvest House Publishers, 2008.
[2] Bruno, Bonnie. *When God Steps In: Stories of Everyday Grace.* Cincinnati: Standard Publishing, 2007.
[3] Elliot, Elisabeth. *Quest for Love: True Stories of Passion and Purity.* Grand Rapids: Fleming H. Revell, 1996.
[7] Douglas, Charles Noel, ed. *Forty Thousand Quotations: Prose and Poetical,* New York: Halcyon House, 1917; *Bartleby.com,* 2012.

Chapter 5: Obstacles

[1] Cragg, Sheila. *A Woman's Walk with God: A Daily Guide for Prayer and Spiritual Growth.* Wheaton, Illinois: Crossway Books, 1996.

Chapter 7: Sin and Forgiveness

[1] Tileston, Mary Wilder, ed. *Joy and Strength for the Pilgrim's Day*. Boston: Little, Brown, and Co., 1901.

Chapter 9: Endurance and Perseverance

[1] Meyer, Joyce. *Never Give Up!* Nashville: Faith Words, 2009.
[2] Simpson, Albert Benjamin. *Days of Heaven upon Earth*. New York: Christian Alliance Publishing Co., 1897.

Chapter 10: Spiritual Path and Spiritual Journey

[1] Henry, Matthew. *An Exposition of the Old and New Testament*. Volume II. London: Joseph Ogle Robinson, 1828.
[2] Holowaty, Nancy. "Nancy Holowaty." Posted December 16, 2012. *I Like to Waste My Time*. http://iliketowastemytime.com/taxonomy/term/559. Accessed July 7, 2013.
[3] Chambers, Oswald. *My Utmost for His Highest*. Grand Rapids: Discovery House Publishers, 1992.

Chapter 13: God's Will vis-à-vis Free Will

[1] Lewis, C.S. *The Problem of Pain*. London: Fount Paperbacks, 1984.

Chapter 14: Healing

[1] Zelenka, Cheryl. "Bride of Christ Jesus." Posted May 9, 2013. *Facing Trials*. http://facingtrials.com/bride-of-christ-jesus/. Accessed July 8, 2013.

Chapter 15: God's Plan and Purpose

[1] Tozer, Aiden W. *The Root of the Righteous*. Camp Hill, Pennsylvania: WingSpread, 1955.

Chapter 16: Control

[1] Ten Boom, Corrie. *The Hiding Place*. Grand Rapids: Chosen Books, 1971.

Chapter 17: Worry and Anxiety

[1] Clarkson, Sally. "What Mother Can Find Favor with God?" Posted December 18, 2012. *I Take Joy*. http://www.itakejoy.com/what-mother-can-find-favor-with-god/. Accessed July 7, 2013.

Chapter 18: Hope

[1] Marshall, Catherine. "The Door of Hope." Posted on May 13, 2011. *The Enchanting Cottage*. http://enchantingcottage.blogspot.com/2011/05/door-of-hope.html. Accessed July 7, 2013.

[2] Arthur, Kay. "Kay Arthur Quotes." *oChristian.com*. http://christian-quotes.ochristian.com/Kay-Arthur-Quotes/page-2.shtml. Accessed July 7, 2013.

Chapter 20: Walking with the Spirit of God

[1] *Dictionary.com*. http://dictionary.reference.com/browse/resist?s=t. Accessed July 8, 2013.

[2] "Guy H King Quotes." *searchquotes.com*. http://www.searchquotes.com/quotation/No_one_is_a_firmer_believer_in_the_power_of_prayer_than_the_devil%3B_not_that_he_practices_it,_but_he_/223066/. Accessed July 7, 2013.

Made in the USA
Lexington, KY
12 December 2013